Photographing Nature

FLOWERS

Heather Angel MSc FIIP FRPS

First Published 1975

FOUNTAIN PRESS, ARGUS BOOKS LIMITED
Station Road, Kings Langley, Hertfordshire, England

CONTENTS

INTRODUCTION

Flowers have always been one of the most popular subjects amongst nature photographers. Their diverse colour, shape and form provide unlimited scope for photography – most especially for the close-up enthusiast. There are few places in the world where, at the right season, the photographer will fail to find flowers.

This book aims to encourage both botanists and photographers to try out some new techniques in any available habitat. Alpine flowers hold a special attraction for many photographers, but it is hoped that some readers may be encouraged to turn their attention towards photography in the comparatively neglected forest and wetland areas. Although the main emphasis has been placed on the photography of flowers in their natural habitats, studio portraits have been included, because they are an integral part of flower photography. The techniques in this book refer almost exclusively to wild flowers, but they can be applied equally well to cultivated flowers.

Throughout, a basic knowledge of photography has been assumed, so that the maximum space could be devoted to describing techniques relating to all aspects of flower photography. The photographic terms used in this book are, however, defined in Appendix A and a summary of the equipment and accessories for flower photography – both in the field and indoors – can be found in Appendix B. This book continues to adopt the practical approach of the other titles in this series, and photographs have been included to illustrate most of the techniques. All the monochrome, and most of the colour photographs were taken with a Hasselblad camera. The rest of the colour plates were taken with a Nikkormat camera.

Flowers present an array of subjects and designs for both a scientific and an artistic approach to their photography.

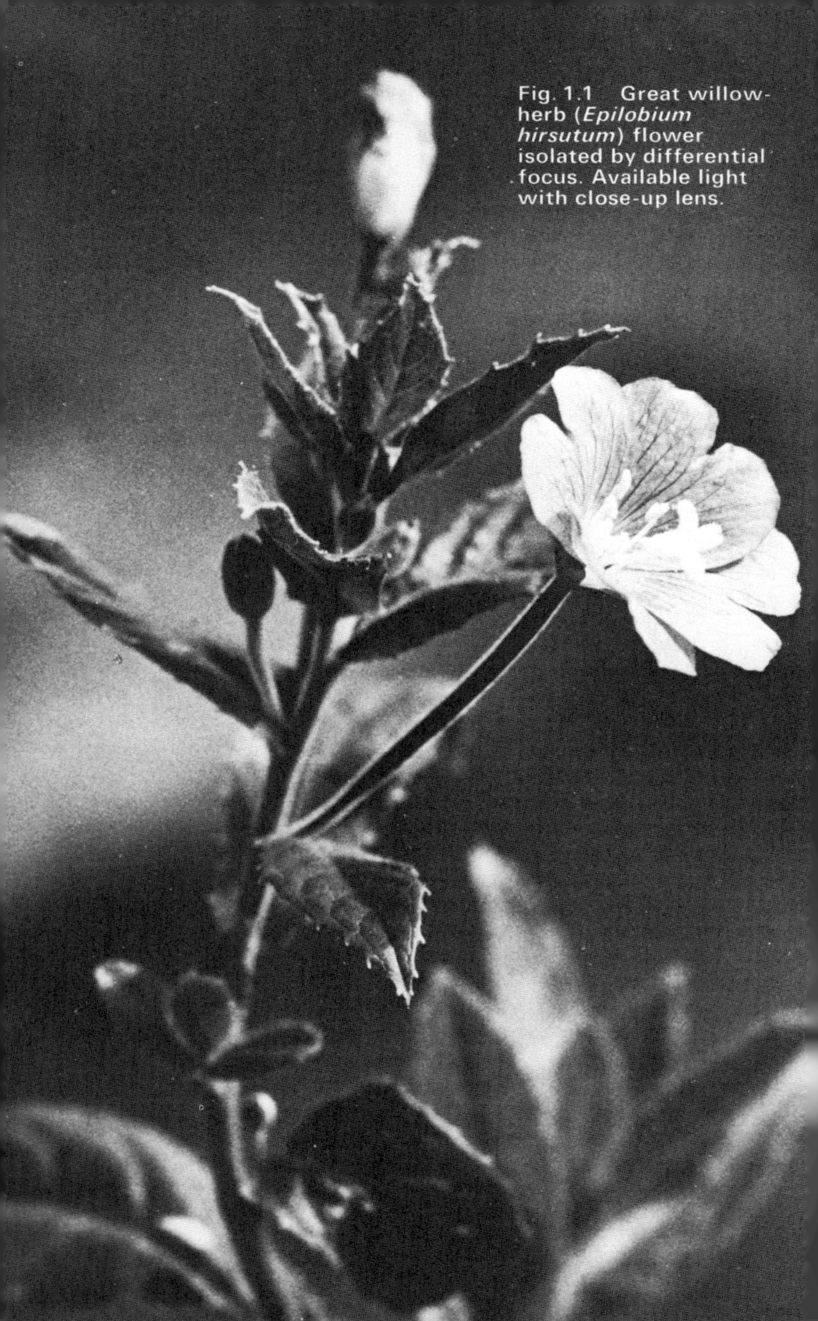

Fig. 1.1 Great willow-herb (*Epilobium hirsutum*) flower isolated by differential focus. Available light with close-up lens.

Plant photography is not always easy and straightforward. It is relatively simple to take a striking colour photograph of a large, brightly coloured bloom; but any plant with flowers which are either small, or spread out on tall spikes, or which blend in with their surroundings, produces problems that can often result in disappointing photographs. Plants are static and this leads to the tendency for photograph after photograph to be taken with the flower or spike of flowers positioned centrally in the frame. No natural history subject – least of all a flower – can be considered non-photogenic. It is up to the photographer to use a whole array of techniques to introduce life into his pictures – techniques ranging from choice of lens, critical lighting, differential focus, to dramatic close-ups and time-lapse exposures.

Striking flower photographs are achieved both by advance reading and planning as well as by chance discovery. Knowing when and where to find a particular species, coupled with a critical eye for selecting a typical, but none the less photogenic specimen, are essential ingredients contributing towards a good flower picture.

Apart from the enjoyment and aesthetic value of flower photographs taken in the field, they have many practical uses. They can provide a record of the species which appear month by month throughout the year in a particular habitat. Colour transparencies of flowers are particularly useful to botanical artists working 'out of season' and also to botanists working in conjunction with dried herbarium specimens. More and more popular floras are utilizing colour transparencies for the colour plates. Providing the reproduction in the original processing, as well as in the final printing, represents an accurate colour rendering, colour photographs are helpful for identifying many, but certainly not all species.

Locations

In any given habitat, there are so many potential subjects, that it is possible to work quite haphazardly, photographing whatever catches the eye. Such a hit and miss approach will tend to result in a collection of unrelated photographs. The length of time during which a particular species flowers is given in advanced floras, but the exact time will vary from season to season and also with both the latitude and the altitude of the location. Since the flowering time of any plant is limited, it is important to be in the right place at the right time.

The locality is every bit as important as the timing. For widespread or especially striking plants, knowing an area of their typical habitat will be sufficient; but many plants have a very limited distribution. There is nothing more frustrating having been given vague directions of how to find a locality with the assurance 'You can't miss it', to find that *nothing* tallies with the directions. It is therefore essential to have not only the Ordnance Survey grid reference (in Britain) but also descriptive landmarks and a sketch map.

Some problems of photographing flowers are common to all habitats, while others relate to specific habitats. Mountain, forest and wetland habitats each present special difficulties, which are covered in detail in separate chapters. When photographing a plant in the field, take at least one exposure showing it in relation to its habitat. This ecological approach is invaluable for providing comparative scale of natural objects such as leaves, as well as a clue towards the identification of the plant. Avoid photographing damaged or atypical specimens. It is both a waste of time and film recording a tatty plant unless it is rare, or specific damage by pests or parasites is required. Good flower photography is a compromise between selecting an intact specimen and utilizing to the best advantage the light and shadow to illustrate specific features of each particular plant.

Open-grown flowers receive the maximum amount of light, but coastal and montane regions particularly, are exposed to plenty of wind. Even on an apparently 'windless' day, short gusts can still shake a flower sufficiently to ruin an exposure. Similarly, photography of flowers on the verges of roads carrying a continuous stream of traffic, is almost impossible, due to the gusty air currents produced by passing vehicles. Various ways of combating wind are given on page 37. Plants growing along the banks of sunken roads or on high walls may be inaccessible for close-up photography without the use of a stepladder. Coastal flowers present the additional problem of the salt-laden atmosphere which is a hazard to marine photography in general. Protecting the lens coating from the spray with a haze filter should be standard practice, even on calm days.

Basic equipment

Cameras Photographs of flowers can be taken on any type of camera, but the most versatile is the single lens reflex camera

(SLR) with an interchangeable lens system. 35mm models are more popular than 6 × 6cm SLR cameras, mainly owing to their competitive prices and lighter weights, but also because of the through-the-lens (TTL) metering facility now available on most models, which is discussed more fully on page 17.

Twin lens reflex (TLR) cameras are still favoured by some plant photographers who prefer working with a format larger than 35mm. TLR cameras provide a cheaper alternative to the 6 × 6cm SLR cameras, but like non-reflex cameras, with close-ups they present the problem of parallax error. This is the discrepancy between what the separate viewfinder (on viewfinder cameras) or the separate lens (on TLR cameras) sees and what the taking lens includes within its field of view. In distant photographs this can be ignored, but in close-ups it must be corrected for by slightly raising the camera. The amount of adjustment can be predetermined by photographing a numbered grid and noting the discrepancy between the area viewed and that photographed. Cards showing the extent of these areas can then be made for different magnifications.

In SLR cameras the photographer sees through the taking lens via the mirror and the viewfinder, exactly what will be reproduced on the film. Therefore for photographing flowers in close-up, an SLR camera will be simpler and so preferable to use than all other types of camera.

Choice of lens One of the major advantages of SLR (and some TLR) cameras, is the option of interchangeable lenses of different focal lengths. Lenses for SLR cameras either have fully automatic diaphragms (FAD) or preset diaphragms (PD). FAD lenses are quicker to use, but they are not as essential for photographing flowers as moving animals.

Flowers can be photographed exclusively with a standard lens, but both longer and shorter focal length lenses can sometimes be used to advantage. A wide angle lens is especially useful for illustrating plants in relation to their habitats while still showing all their major features (Plates 4 and 6 and Figs. 1.2 and 2.1). A long focus lens is ideal for photographing inaccessible plants (Plate 1 and Fig. 1.3), for concentrating attention on part of a plant, and for isolating a flower from its background (page 11).

The most useful lens for close-up photography however, is the specially designed macro lens, which has its own built-in extension. The focal length of a 35mm format macro lens is usually the

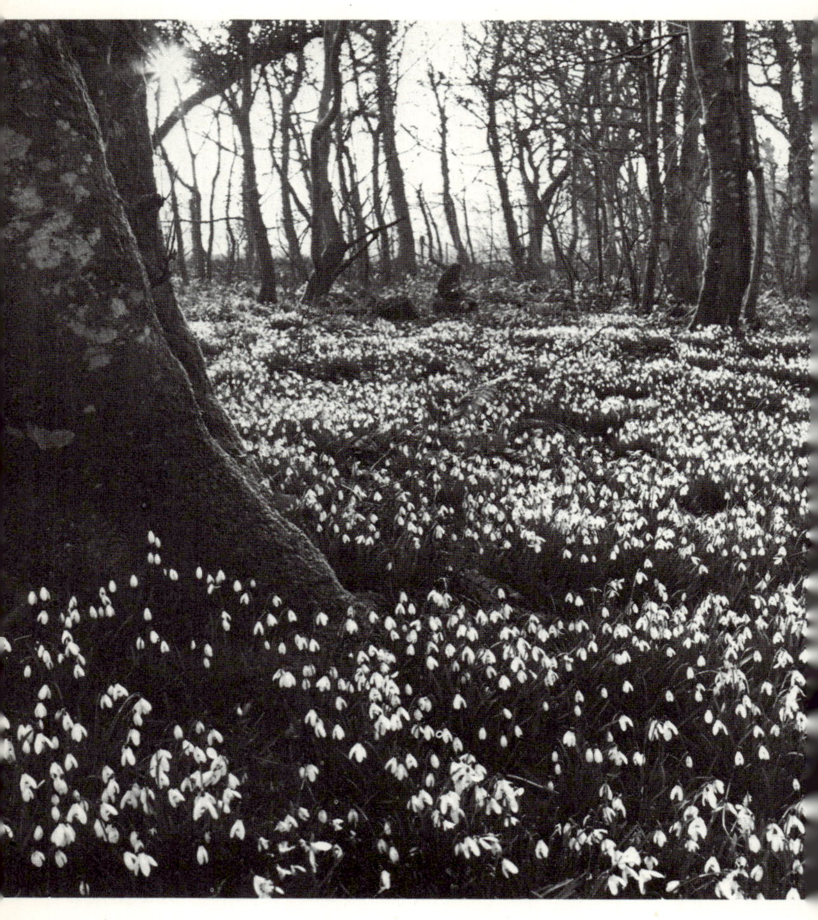

Fig. 1.2 A carpet of snowdrops (*Galanthus nivalis*). Available diffuse lighting with wide angle lens.

same as the standard lens (50–55mm). These purpose-built lenses are, however, more expensive than a standard lens.

Camera supports It is important to select carefully the camera viewpoint to show off each subject to its best advantage. For example, the form of a creeping plant will be seen more clearly from directly overhead (Fig. 2.3), than from the side. In contrast, a low viewpoint may help to isolate a tall plant against the sky (page 11). Although camera supports are more easily used for photographing flowers *in situ* than for active animals, they are not used often enough by plant photographers. Consistent high quality photographs – particularly close-ups – cannot be achieved by hand-held cameras. A firm support will not only eliminate any chance of camera shake, but will also ensure critical composition and focusing so that the maximum depth of field is gained (page 18).

The type of camera support will determine the camera viewpoint, which in turn will affect the perspective of the flower. The camera support must be rigid. A weak support, especially a tripod with legs which are prone to collapse, is a waste of time. A conventional waist level tripod is not ideal, since although it is useful for photographing habitats and tall plants, it is unsuitable for taking low growing plants. A tripod with a minimum leg length of about a third of a metre will be more versatile. Even greater flexibility will be gained from a tripod with a reversible centre column, so that the camera can be mounted close to the ground. Since the ground is rarely level, a tripod with fully adjustable legs will be a great asset.

The serious flower photographer is never without some form of miniature camera support. For low level photography, either a table top tripod or a ground spike are invaluable and much lighter than a standard tripod. Several different kinds of table top tripods are available on the market; some more robust than others. One especially neat, lightweight and easily adjustable model is the German Photo Käfer (Photo Beetle). The pair of legs at each end of the main plate can be locked at a variety of angles and tucked away underneath when not in use. Fine adjustments can be made to the camera angle if an additional ball-and-socket head is attached to the main plate. Ground spikes are rarely marketed, but they are relatively easy and cheap to make. A metal tent peg, or any tapering piece of metal about 10 centimetres long, can be used as the spike. Horizontal arms welded to the top will prevent the spike slipping sideways in soft ground. Finally, a small ball-and-socket head is attached to the top. A ground spike has few

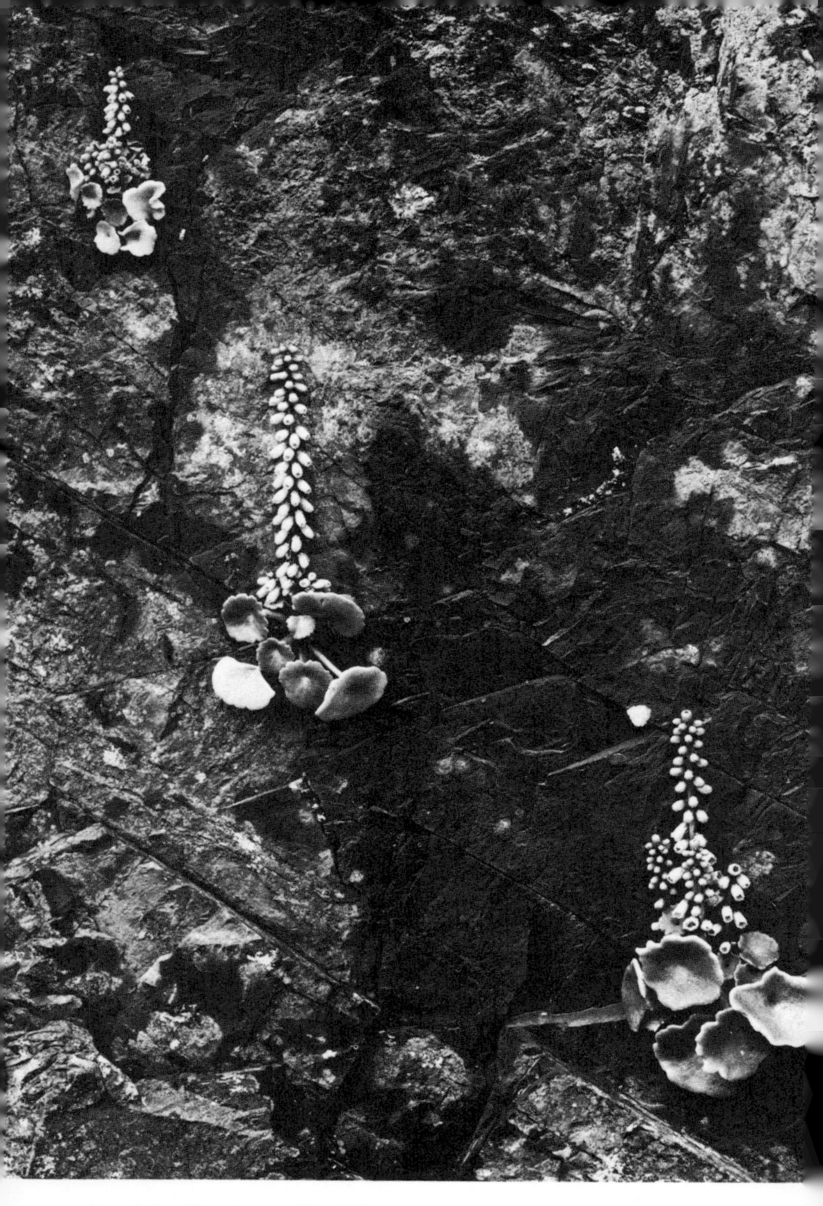

Fig. 1.3 Navelwort (*Umbilicus rupestris*) on a high wall beside the sea. Available diffuse lighting with long focus lens.

limitations apart from rocky or stony ground. A lowpod is simply a piece of wood with an attached ball-and-socket head. It can be used only on flattish ground, and so is more limited than the ground spike, even if wedges or stones are inserted underneath to steady it.

'Gardening'

Before setting up the camera, look critically at the flower and its immediate surroundings. Is it a typical specimen, or is it damaged or eaten? Does it merge in with its surroundings? Is the available lighting adequate, or will flashlight be needed? Do background objects behind the zone of sharp focus conflict with and so detract from the subject? Is an essential detail obscured by plants or by leaf litter? Answers to these questions will determine the camera viewpoint and the choice of lens. Once the viewpoint has been chosen, the flower can then be viewed critically through an SLR camera, to see if any 'gardening' is necessary. This involves the careful removal from the foreground or the background of distracting objects such as bleached grass and bracken stems. The aim is to show clearly the features of a flower without completely destroying the surrounding vegetation. If the 'gardening' is apparent in the photograph, it has failed. Large branches can temporarily be pulled back and held outside the field of view with plastic-coated garden wire.

Isolation from background

On colour film, large brightly coloured flowers or compact heads of small florets stand out from their immediate surroundings (Plates 1, 5, 7 and 8). However, flowers which blend with their background or which have inaccessible distracting objects behind them, will require one of several techniques to isolate them. The use of these techniques clearly conflicts with the requirements of ecological photography of flowers, in which the aim is to include as much information as possible about the background.

Sky and water provide natural backgrounds for some plants. Plants growing well above ground level or at high altitudes can often be photographed against the sky (Fig. 1.4). Parts of tall plants can be taken from a low camera viewpoint against the sky using a medium long focus lens. Conversely, a higher viewpoint is usually needed to isolate plants growing alongside water.

A polarizing filter may help to increase the contrast between a flower and the background sky or water. For maximum effect of

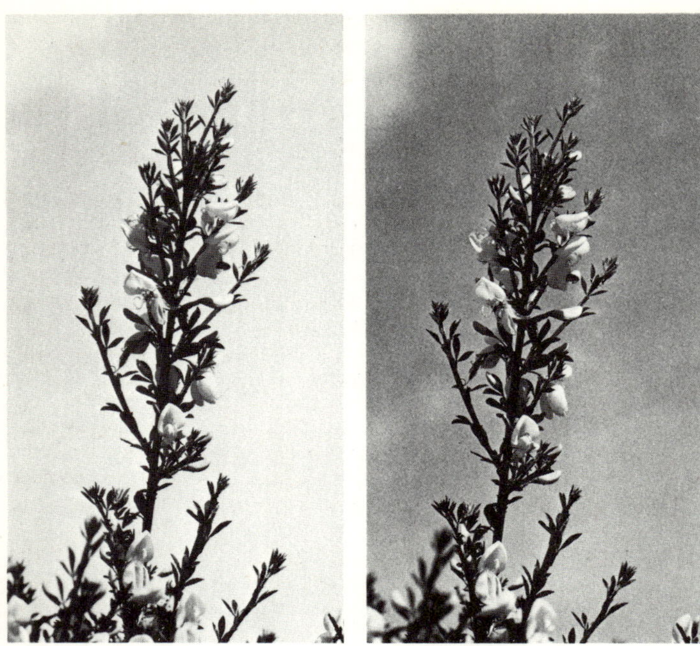

Fig. 1.4 Broom (*Sarothamnus scoparius*) in direct sunlight against the sky without (left) and with (right) a polarizing filter. Long focus lens.

darkening blue sky, a polarizing filter must be used at right angles to the sun (Fig. 1.4). The precise effect of full or partial polarization can be seen with an SLR camera, and on TTL models the exposure appropriately adjusted. A polarizing filter is the only filter which will darken blue sky on both monochrome and colour films without affecting any other colours.

Light and shade can be used to isolate almost any kind of erect plant growing in any habitat. The opportunities may be limited; a shaft of sunlight streaming through a woodland will spotlight a plant for a very few minutes. It is therefore essential to work quickly, before the shaft of sunlight moves on. Examples shown of brightly lit subjects photographed against dark shadow are the deadly nightshade (Plate 3), the teasel (Plate 18) and the Kashmiri drug plant (Fig. 2.4). Plate 3 was a lucky picture, for just as I arrived at where the plant was growing inside a beechwood, the sun shone on to it through a break in the overhead canopy. The teasel, growing on a stream bank, was highlighted by the sun late in the day against the trees growing along the opposite bank. Figure 2.4 was also taken late in the day when the sun was low in the sky.

If both the subject and the background are in full sunlight, a background shadow can be cast quite independently of the weather conditions, by a convenient object – such as a companion or a gadget bag. Flashlight can also be used to separate a flower from its background. The intensity of flashlight falls off by the square of the distance. The background therefore does not have to lie very far behind the subject for it not to be illuminated and to appear completely black. Some plant photographers dislike this stark 'nocturnal' appearance to a flash field photograph and avoid it at all costs; but there are occasions when flash can be used to produce a dramatic effect, as for example in Plate 23. Flash was used here both to provide sparkle to the hoar frost and to eliminate the distracting criss-crossing stems of shorter plants growing beneath the dead hogweed head in the roadside verge. This pattern picture does not attempt to illustrate the entire plant or its surrounding habitat.

Flowers can also be isolated by photographing them against the light so that they become silhouetted against a brightly lit background. This is not such a suitable technique for isolating flowers as trees, since flower colour is a fundamental character.

Differential focus is when a limited zone only appears sharp and in focus in a photograph. It is a technique often used unwittingly in flower close-ups, in which the limited depth of field will throw the background out of focus. As mentioned above (page 11), distracting out of focus objects often spoil flower photographs. So for differential focus to be successful, the background must not conflict or compete with the subject, but harmonize with it by either appearing as uniform in tone and colour, or as a mosaic of sombre tones or colours (Plates 1, 2, 7, 9 and 13).

The exact depth of field (page 18) can be critically viewed beforehand by manually stopping down the lens to the preselected aperture, or by depressing the preview button on FAD lenses. It can be increased either by stopping down the lens diaphragm to a smaller aperture, or by moving the camera further away from the subject, but at the expense of decreasing the image size. Conversely, the depth of field is decreased either by opening up the aperture or by increasing the magnification.

A long focus lens is rarely used by flower photographers; but a medium long focus lens such as 135mm on a 35mm format, can be extremely useful for achieving differential focus of larger flowers (Plates 1 and 7). After rain or beside stretches of water and when photographing looking up through open shrubs or trees, check for distracting highlights appearing behind the subject plane. A predominant background montage of polygonal or circular shapes (the outline of the diaphragm) may be ideal for an audio-visual performance, but is not the aim of a critical natural history close-up. Small highlights can, however, be a subtle way of indicating a wet habitat, as shown in Plate 5. In Plate 2, gorse, a common heathland plant, has a pink mosaic behind it suggesting the heather with which it is typically associated.

Filters When using monochrome films, filters can be used to increase the contrast between uniformly toned but different coloured flowers and background. Contrast filters, which are strongly coloured, lighten an object of the same colour and darken objects of other colours, especially the complementary colour. Thus either a green or a red filter can be used to increase the contrast and so isolate a red flower from surrounding green leaves, both of which would otherwise be reproduced in the same grey tone. A green filter will lighten the leaves and darken the flower, while a red filter will lighten the flower and darken the foliage in the final print. Gelatin filters which are cheap but scratch easily, are ideal for initial experiments. Glass filters, which can be screwed on to the front of the lens, are preferable for long term use. All filters should be kept just as clean as the lens itself.

Since contrast filters cut out some of the light from reaching the film, an increase in exposure will be necessary. This is quite simple with cameras having a TTL metering system. The use of much paler filters with colour films, is discussed on pages 21 and 45.

Artificial backgrounds It is possible to eliminate completely a confusing background by simply inserting a board behind a flower. However, any plain coloured background – even if it is blue or green – will appear quite unnatural due to the uniformity of the colour or tone. Tonal uniformity does not occur in nature; even a clear blue sky grades in intensity. A possible solution might be to use a colour photographic print of the relevant habitat – in the same way as aquarists use photographic weedy backgrounds for their fish tanks. Even then, critical appraisal of the direction of the light falling on the subject, would have to be made to ensure that the two-dimensional photographic reproduction closely simulated the light and shadows of the natural three-dimensional background. My own feeling is that it ruins a spontaneous approach to *in situ* flower photography, and that the use of an artificial background eliminates any suggestion of the natural surroundings, so that the result is a record rather than a true nature photograph.

An artificial background can, however, be invaluable for clarifying botanical details, especially of rare plants which must not be collected for photography indoors. Plain grey or buff backgrounds are ideal for taking anatomical flower photographs in the field, since they will not throw an unnatural colour cast on to the flower. Record photographs are more useful for artist's reference if a rule is placed alongside the flower.

Getting in close

One of the delights of flower photography is the pleasure gained from taking and viewing close-ups. Many of the illustrations in this book show flowers in close-up, both in the field and indoors. This approach to flower photography should be used to supplement pictures of the entire plant in its habitat, rather than to replace them.

Close-up photography begins at the shortest camera-to-subject distance which a standard (not a macro) lens can be focused without an accessory, down to life size or 1:1 reproduction. The term macrophotography is more appropriate for magnifications of over 1:1. Because close-up photographs can be enlarged to greater than life size, original macrophotographs have been distinguished from close-ups by the letter M at the end of the caption.

The aim of natural history close-ups should be to get the subject sharply defined. This does not necessarily mean that the entire flower spike should be sharp all over; greater impact and just as much information may be possible by focusing on a single flower and throwing the rest out of focus.

A macro lens, already described on page 7, is the quickest way of getting in close. It is ideal for the photographer specializing in close-ups, since the minimum aperture is usually smaller (f/32 on the Micro-Nikkor) than on an equivalent standard lens, although the maximum aperture is also smaller (f/3.5 on the Micro-Nikkor).

Close-up lenses Supplementary or close-up lenses can be mounted like filters on the front of the camera lens. With the advantages of cheapness and lightness, they are quick to use and are the only way

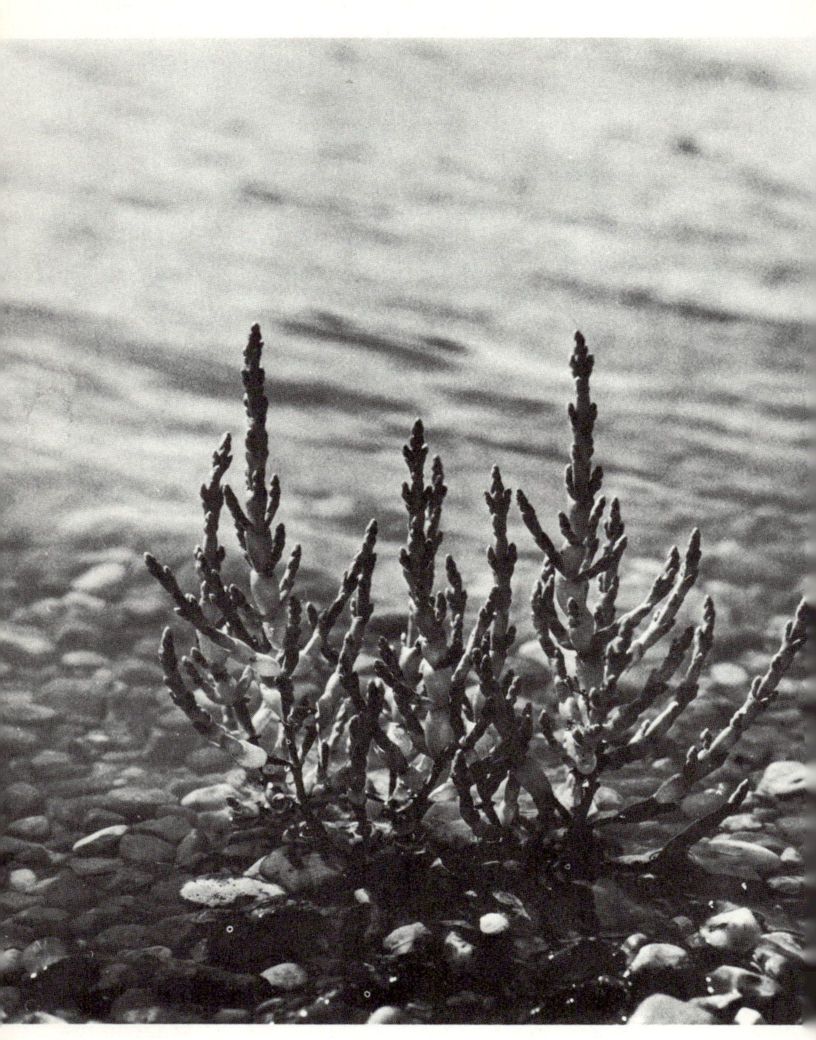

Fig. 1.5 Glasswort (*Salicornia* sp.) isolated against water. Against the light, using close-up lens.

of taking close-ups with fixed lens cameras. A close-up lens is comparable with the spectacle lens required by a far-sighted person to see near objects. It reduces the focal length of the camera lens, but it does not significantly reduce the light reaching the film, and so no exposure correction has to be made. However, there can be overall loss in definition – especially with cheap close-up lenses – unless small apertures such as f/8 or f/11 are used.

The power of a close-up lens is quoted in dioptres as used by opticians. Convex lenses (including close-up lenses) are referred to in terms of a positive dioptre figure, whereas concave lenses are designated by a minus dioptre figure. Close-up lenses are manufactured covering a range of dioptres; a + 2 dioptre lens magnifying twice as much as a + 1 dioptre lens. It is possible, but not recommended, to increase the magnification by using combinations of close-up lenses.

Extension tubes and bellows can be used on cameras with interchangeable lenses. By increasing the camera extension, they increase the distance the light has to travel to reach the film plane, so that an exposure adjustment has to be made (see below).

Extension tubes are cheaper than bellows, but more expensive than close-up lenses. A full set of tubes provides a limited combination of extensions. Bellows have the advantages of a continuous focusing range, coupled with the possibility of magnifications greater than the maximum of 1:1 possible with a full set of extension tubes and a 50mm lens. Only a few bellows, but most extension tubes, automatically close down to the preselected aperture as the shutter is released. Non-auto tubes or bellows are not so limiting for photographing flowers as active insects.

Exposure A correctly exposed negative or transparency is obtained by selecting the right combination of aperture and shutter speed, for a given film speed and a particular light intensity. Incorrect exposure when using extension tubes or bellows is one of the common faults in close-up photographs; but once the principles are known and understood there should be no problems. The TTL metering now becoming widespread in 35mm SLR cameras removes most of the headache of determining the exposure increase for close-ups. However, cameras which have a 'full screen' metering system make no allowances for a subject which is lighter or darker than the rest of the field of view. For such subjects, a camera with a 'spot' meter will be more accurate. Even then, because TTL meters measure light reflected from the subject, they will not be so accurate for determining the exposure of a small pale flower against a dark background. A separate light meter, fitted with a diffusing cone, will provide a more accurate reading, by measuring the incident light falling on the subject. For TTL metering to succeed, it must be used intelligently. It is much quicker to use than a separate light meter and it is the only way of ensuring a final check on the exposure, immediately before the shutter is released. This is especially useful on days when the sun is constantly disappearing and reappearing behind clouds.

For cameras without TTL metering, the exposure increase must be calculated and the aperture and shutter speed adjusted accordingly. Unfortunately, instructions supplied with the extension tubes or bellows are often misleading. The first important factor to grasp is that the amount of exposure increase will vary according to the amount of extension used and also with the focal length of the lens. A simple method is to take a light reading of the subject with a light meter, and select an aperture as a basis for determining by how much the lens aperture needs to be opened.

$$\text{aperture/f number to be used} = \text{aperture taken from light meter reading} \times \frac{\text{focal length of lens (in mm)}}{\text{focal length of lens} + \text{extension (in mm)}}$$

If a complete set of extension tubes (50mm) is used with a standard lens on a 35mm format camera, the distance from the lens to the film plane is doubled from 50 to 100mm. As a result of the inverse square law (page 13) the amount of light reaching the film is quartered and not halved, so that the aperture must be opened up by two full stops. If the original exposure is $^1/_{60}$ second at f/8, either the aperture must be opened up to f/4 or the shutter speed reduced to $^1/_{15}$ second. Opening up the lens aperture also reduces the depth of field, so the latter alternative may be preferable if the plant is not moving.

Depth of field In close-up photography the depth of field – the zone of sharp focus in front of and behind the exact plane on which the lens is focused – is limited. Not only is critical focusing essential, but also a clear understanding is needed of how the depth of field can be varied. The aim of natural history close-ups is usually to achieve the maximum depth of field. However, as mentioned on page 13, reduction of the depth of field may be needed to isolate the subject from its surroundings by differential focus.

The depth of field can be increased by using a shorter focal length lens from the same camera position, which will alter the perspective of a photograph as well. It can also be increased by moving further away from the subject and thereby decreasing the image size. For most close-up work the depth of field is increased by 'stopping down' to smaller (f/11 or f/16) rather than using larger (f/4 or f/5.6) apertures. Stopping a lens down increases the depth of field on both sides of the plane of focus, but twice as much behind as in front. Therefore, to achieve the optimum depth of field with close-ups, the camera should be focused a short distance behind the part of a flower nearest to the camera, so that most, if not all, of the flower lies within the zone of sharp focus when the lens is stopped down. The extent of the depth of field for a given magnification and lens aperture can be seen either by manually stopping down the lens or by depressing the special preview button. At magnifications of 1:1 (life size) the depth of field is almost the same on either side of the plane of focus.

Lighting

To both pictorial and landscape photographers, the direction (front, side or back) and the type (diffuse or direct) of lighting is crucial to the success of their pictures. The nature photographer, however, is so often emotionally involved with the subject (especially if it is a rarity which has taken a lot of time and effort to locate) that lighting tends to be unconsidered. So much more enjoyment will be gained from flower photography if careful thought is given to how the available lighting can be used to show off the flower to its best advantage. Photographing every flower lit by sunlight or flashlight from in front, just to add another tick to a check list, shows lack of imagination.

Available lighting is preferable for most *in situ* flower photographs. Obvious exceptions to this generalization are colour photographs taken in dark woodlands and extreme close-ups in general. Days with light cloud cover producing diffuse lighting are ideal for photographing the white and pastel-coloured flowers described on page 45. Similarly, deep throated flowers, such as the bromeliad in Plate 16, will have details in the centre obscured by shadows cast from direct side lighting. Other examples of *in situ* photographs taken by diffuse available lighting can be seen in Plates 5, 6 and 12 and Figs. 1.2, 1.3, 2.2 and 4.3.

Direct side or overhead lighting is useful for conveying a sense of depth to a flower through the modelling effect of light and

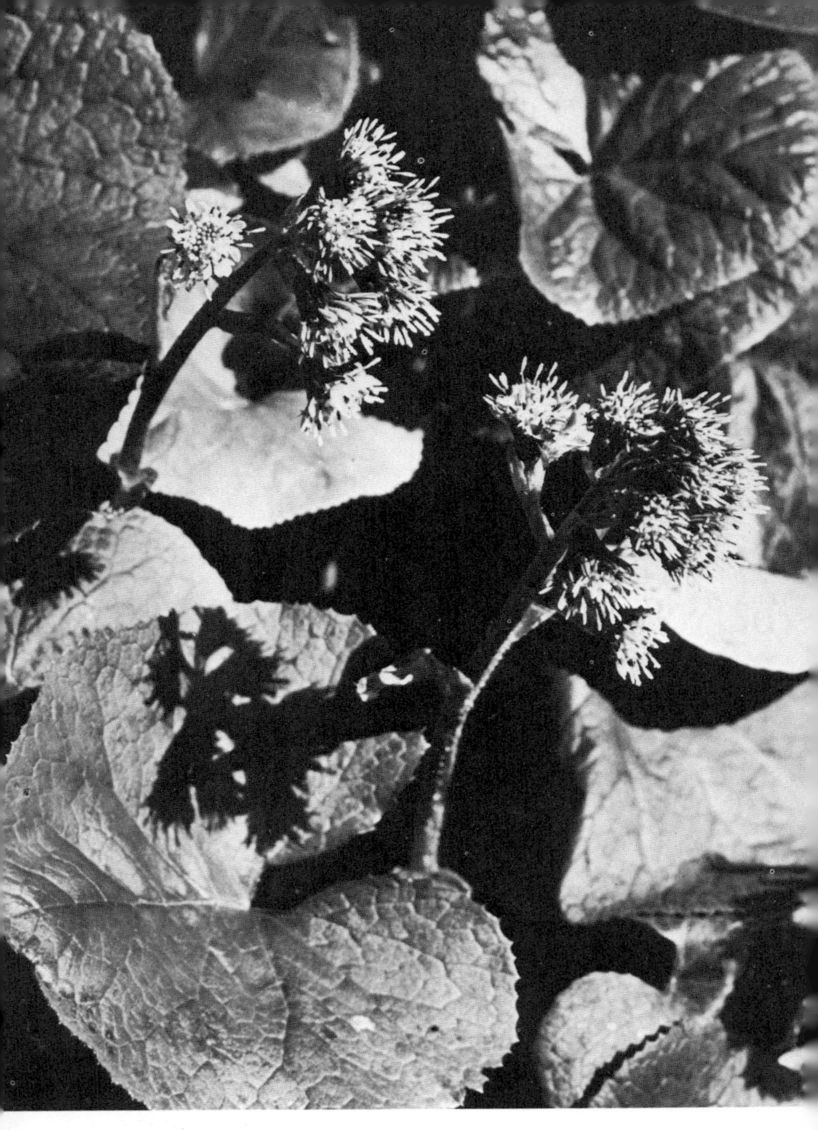

Fig. 1.6 Winter heliotrope (*Petasites fragrans*). Direct sunlight from the side.

shadow (Plate 8). Side lighting can also repeat the shape of a flower by the shadow it casts on the background, on the water in Fig. 4.2 and on the large simple leaves in Fig. 1.6. Side lighting may obscure important details of insignificant flowers, and for these it may be necessary to fill in the shadow area by using a reflector such as a board covered with aluminium cooking foil or a metallic camping mirror. A very effective, large but lightweight light bouncer, is the reusable survival blanket manufactured for campers and hikers, which has an aluminium coating on one side. This blanket makes not only a handy light reflector, but also a serviceable mat for kneeling on damp ground or even a waterproof covering during a sudden rain shower for a camera set up on a tripod.

The photography of plants *contre jour* or against the light, is more often regarded as a pictorial approach; but for some subjects it is ideal. Spiny or hairy stems (Plate 3), fluffy seeds (Plate 14) or any delicate structures (Fig. 2.4) cannot be defined so clearly by any other lighting. It is also useful for showing the venation pattern of translucent leaves (Plate 3). Back lit pictures are usually dramatic and provide a welcome pictorial relief amongst a series of pictures taken by front or side lighting. Always use a lens hood when photographing against the light; this will reduce the chance of flare, caused by the light shining directly on to the front lens element, from spoiling the picture. In an emergency, a hand can be used as a lens hood, but be careful not to get it in the field of view.

Time exposures can be used for photographing flowers in dark locations. When exposures of greater than about 1 second (or shorter than $^{1}/_{1000}$ second) are used, the effective speed of the emulsion is reduced. This reciprocity failure means that when using slow shutter speeds, the correct exposure will be achieved only when an additional exposure increase is made. In practice, long exposures are not to be recommended for colour work, since they cause a shift in the colour balance resulting in unnatural colour reproduction. This is particularly noticeable for greens, which take on a distinct blue cast. The shift can also be seen to a lesser extent by comparing a pair of colour pictures of the same subject taken by diffuse light and by direct sunlight. The 81A correcting filter recommended for 'warming up' colours on overcast days can be tried, but the absence of shadows will make it obvious that the sun was not shining at the time.

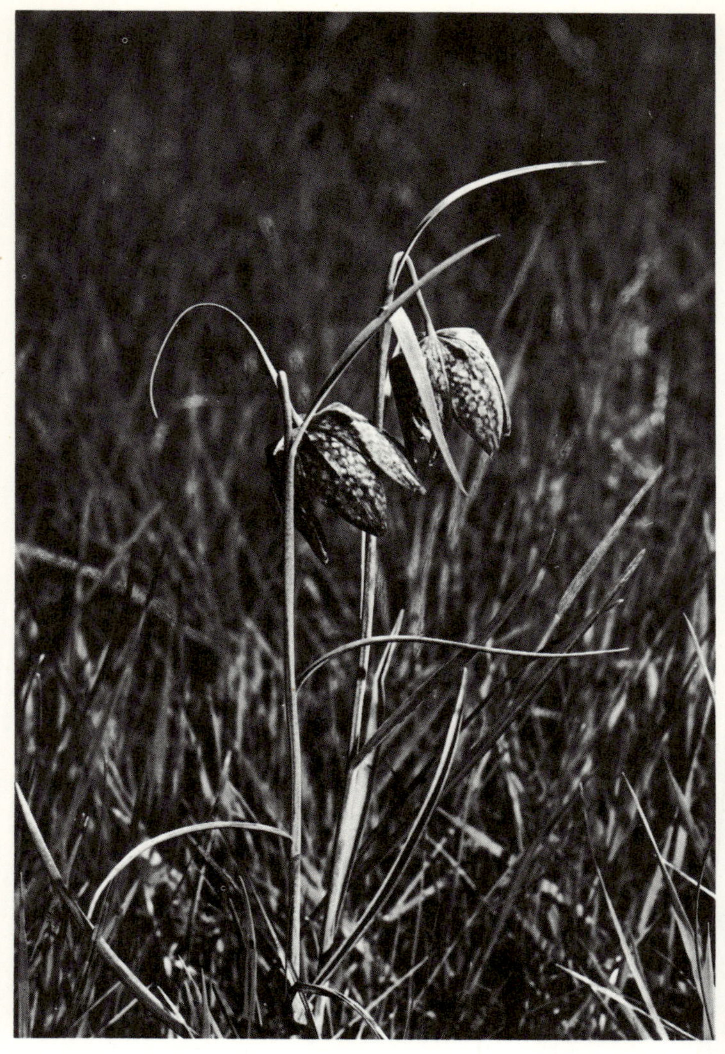

Fig. 1.7 Fritillary (*Fritillaria meleagris*) against the light with synchro-sunlight flash to show pattern on the petals.

For long exposures, the camera must be rigidly supported on a tripod or a ground spike (page 9). Even then, it is advisable to use the mirror lock if one is present, or else to use the delayed action mechanism to reduce vibration. For comparatively short time exposures of 1 second or so, the B setting on the shutter can be used and the time measured with a watch or by counting, the shutter remaining open so long as pressure is maintained on the cable release. For longer exposures, use either a locking cable release or, where present, the T shutter setting (Z on continental shutters) which requires an initial pressure on the release to open the shutter and a second one to close it.

A better solution for colour photography of plants by available light on dull or windy days, is to double rate the film. Before setting the ASA or DIN rating on the light meter or the TTL meter, to double the recommended rate on the film pack, check that the film can be specially processed. Remember to double rate the complete film and to send clear instructions to the processing laboratory that this has been done.

Flashlight can be used for flower photography in the field, but its use should be exceptional rather than the rule. The main disadvantage of flash as the major light source is that it overrides the available light to produce a dark, unlit distant background. Small flowers growing in close association with their background, however, are suitable for flash photography. As already mentioned, flash is essential for colour photography in dark situations, where reciprocity failure will otherwise cause incorrect colour rendering. It is also useful for increasing the depth of field (Plate 19), for isolating the subject from its background (Plate 23) and for arresting movement on a windy day.

The main advantage of flashlight is that its direction can be selected and controlled for each particular subject. Using the flash permanently mounted on the camera will eliminate any possibility of creative lighting. A single flash may produce unacceptable shadows, so that either a second flash or a light bouncer may be needed to relieve them. One or two small electronic flash units can be mounted on to angle brackets attached to the base of the camera. Multiple flash leads are connected to the camera flash socket (X synchronization for electronic flash) by using double or triple adapters. A reflector, including the specially designed flash umbrella, can be useful for bouncing a single flash to give softer light for pale coloured flowers, which so easily become 'burnt-out' by harsh direct flashlight.

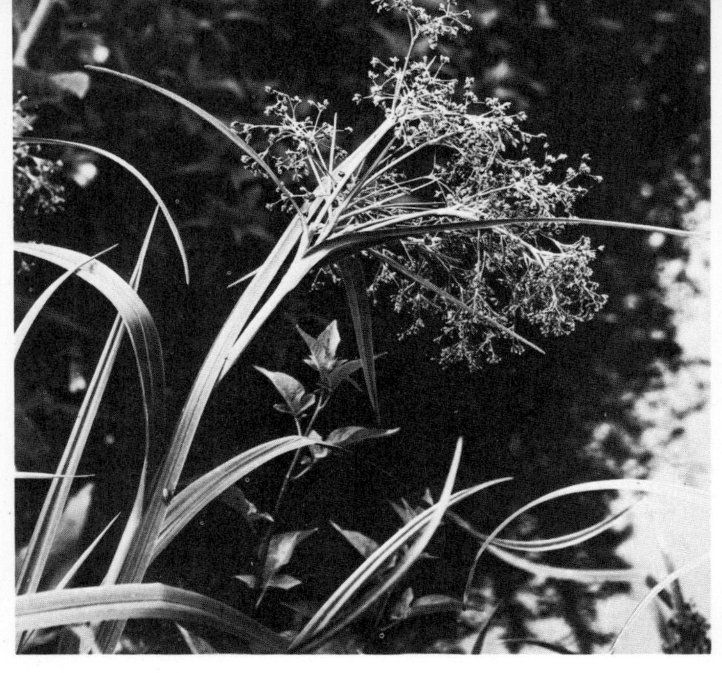

Fig. 1.8 Wood club-rush (*Scirpus sylvaticus*) in a stream bed. Isolated by sun and shadow. Close-up lens.

A camera with a diaphragm or leaf shutter can be synchronized with electronic flash at any speed; but models with a focal plane shutter will synchronize only when the entire frame is exposed at one instant. With some older cameras this is at $^{1}/_{30}$ second, but more recent models synchronize at $^{1}/_{60}$ or even $^{1}/_{125}$ second. It is the speed of the electronic flash, and not the shutter speed, which arrests movement of a subject. When electronic flash is used on a sunny, windy day with a focal plane shutter which has to be synchronized at a slow speed, a blurred or double image can result from both the brief flashlit image and the longer daylit image registering. The numerous factors which affect exposure with flashlight include the film speed, the power of the flash, the flash-to-subject distance, the magnification as well as the tone and texture of the subject and the background. Determination of the correct exposure for flash with close-ups is therefore best done by initial experimentation. Keeping the filmstock, the magnification and the flash-to-subject distance constant, take a series of bracketed exposures of a flower by altering the aperture in one stop increments. Make sure you keep detailed notes, so that the correct exposure can be used as a basis for determining the exposure for darker, paler, larger or smaller subjects. At first, it may simplify matters to mount the flash to one side of the camera on an angle bracket, so that as the camera is moved in towards the subject the flash is also moved forward. This will tend to compensate for a reduction of light intensity with increased extension, and in practice, it may be possible to keep a constant aperture (such as f/16 or f/11) over a range of magnifications.

With increasing experience, flashlight can be used in a more creative way; for example to backlight a hairy plant on an overcast day. If there is no assistant to hold the flash in position behind the subject, mount it on a monopod, a spike or possibly a clamp. Flashlight can also be used to fill in foreground shadows. The technique of using a balanced combination of sunlight and flashlight is known as synchro-sunlight. The shutter speed (remember to use the correct speed for flash synchronization) and aperture are set for the daylight exposure. The guide number for the combination of flash and film speed in use, is then divided by the selected aperture to determine the correct flash-to-subject distance which will provide an intensity equal to the daylight. A slight increase to this distance will produce an acceptable combination whereby the flash fills in, but does not completely override the shadows.

Field notes

If accurate identification of a flower cannot be made on the spot, it is essential that full notes are made in the field at the time. These can either be jotted down into a hard-backed field notebook or dictated into a pocket tape recorder. First note the date, habitat and possibly the microhabitat. Once some experience has been gained in using a field identification guide, specific characters will automatically be noted; for example, members of the cress family (Cruciferae) often can only be identified from their fruits. It is worth noting the flower shape and colour (both inside and outside) as well as the leaf shape. Where do the leaves arise? Do they vary in size along the length of the plant? A hand lens should be regarded as essential to the plant photographer as to the botanist. Accurate measurements taken with a pocket tape measure will be invaluable for confirming the magnifications on the negative or transparency.

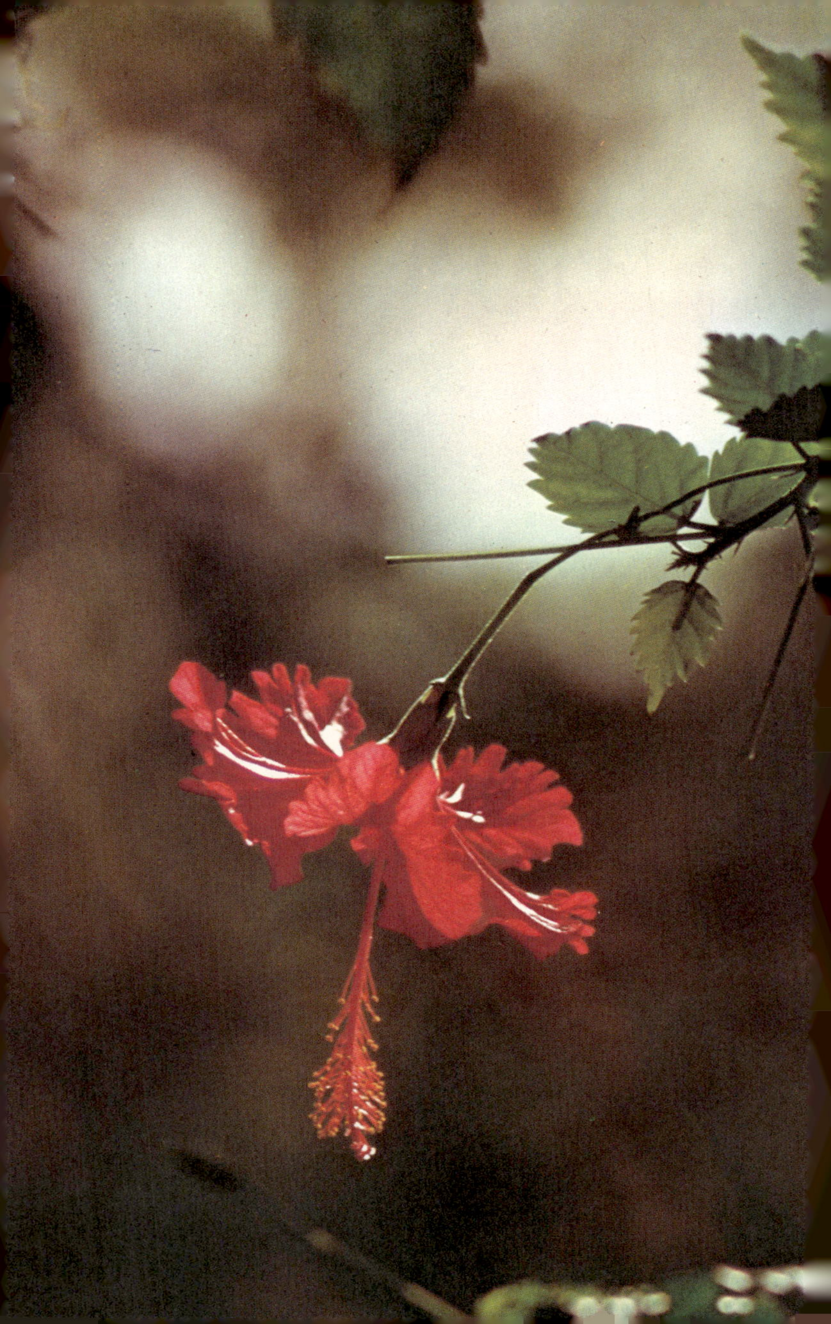

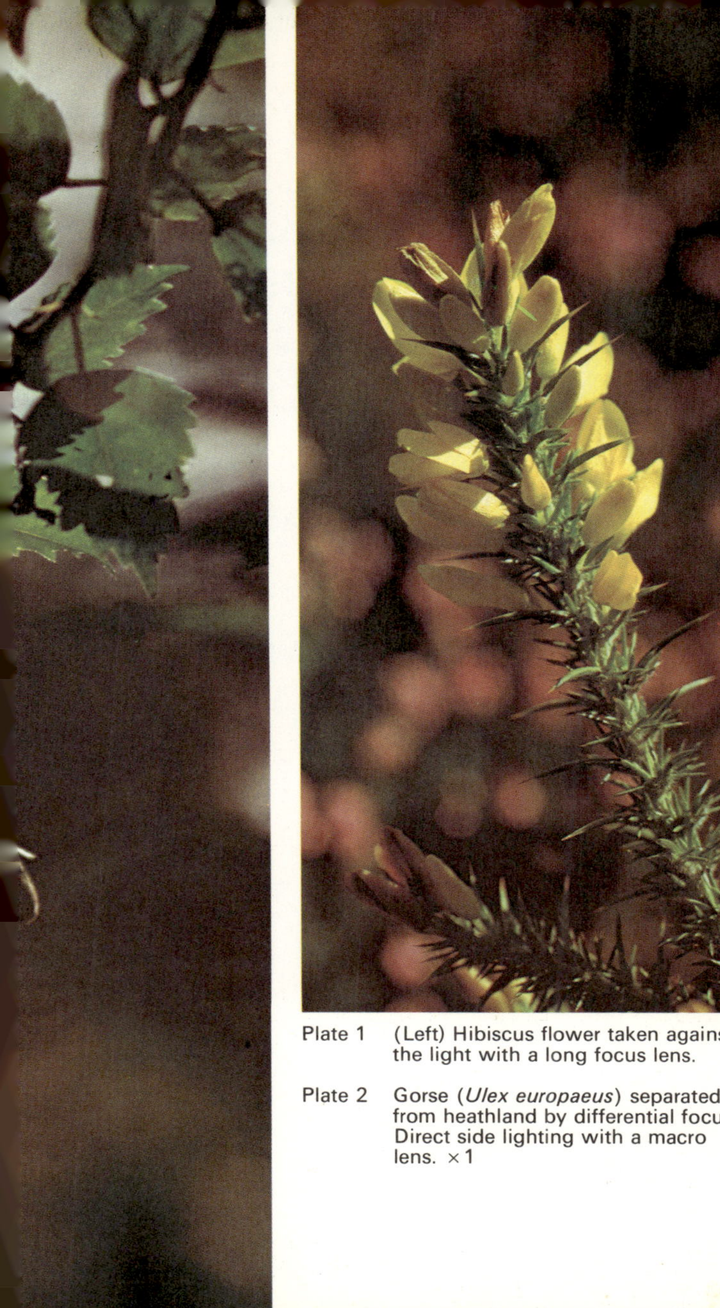

Plate 1 (Left) Hibiscus flower taken against the light with a long focus lens.

Plate 2 Gorse (*Ulex europaeus*) separated from heathland by differential focus. Direct side lighting with a macro lens. ×1

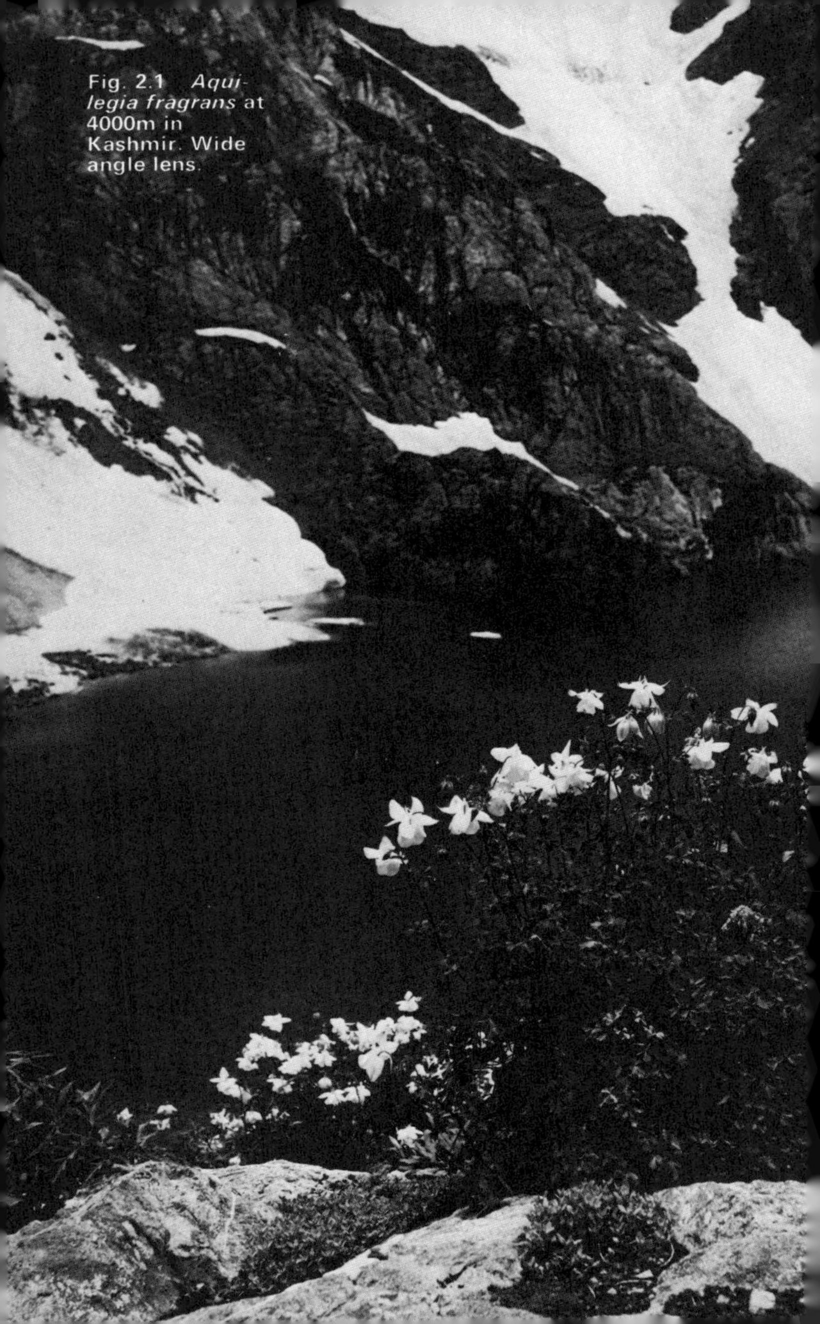

Fig. 2.1 *Aquilegia fragrans* at 4000m in Kashmir. Wide angle lens.

Plants which are more or less restricted to mountains are known as alpines. For centuries, alpine growers have travelled world-wide in search of new plants. Now that some of the more far-flung and remote mountains are becoming accessible to more than a handful of dedicated botanists, it is fortunate that the camera has almost replaced the trowel.

The habitat

The height at which choice alpines grow varies with the climate and the latitude. On a world scale, British mountains are small. But height is not so important as the nature of the underlying soil and the aspect. There is not, for example, a great wealth of plants to be found on the tops of the 1200m high Scottish mountains. *The* area for alpines in Britain is the Scottish Highlands south of the Great Glen, especially the Lawers Range in Perthshire. Ben Lawers (1215m) which is regarded as a botanist's Mecca, is formed from schists and quartzites. It is the basic mica schists which many plants favour in preference to the acidic soils present on most British mountains.

Britain has few endemic alpines. Its alpine flora can be divided into three groups relating to its distribution outside Britain. The *arctics* occur in the Arctic region, including Scandinavia, but not in the European mountain ranges; while the *alpines* occur on the European mountains but not in the Arctic. The majority of British mountain plants are the so-called *arctic-alpines*, which occur both in the Arctic and on some, or all, of the main European mountain ranges. In terms of number of species, the British mountain flora is sparse; about 130 species of ferns and flowering plants grow above 600m. In addition, there are also many plants which grow above 600m, which are not confined to mountains. Some alpines and arctic-alpines can be found growing at sea level in parts of northern Scotland and western Ireland, and there are some coastal plants which can grow on mountains. A much greater variety of alpines occur on the more extensive mountain ranges in continental Europe, Asia and North America. Above the tree-line, alpines are typically low growing, compact or prostrate plants. Their stunted growth is due to the brief growing season – for most of the year they are submerged by a blanket of snow. Long periods of lightness also retard the growth of shoots. In the Arctic region,

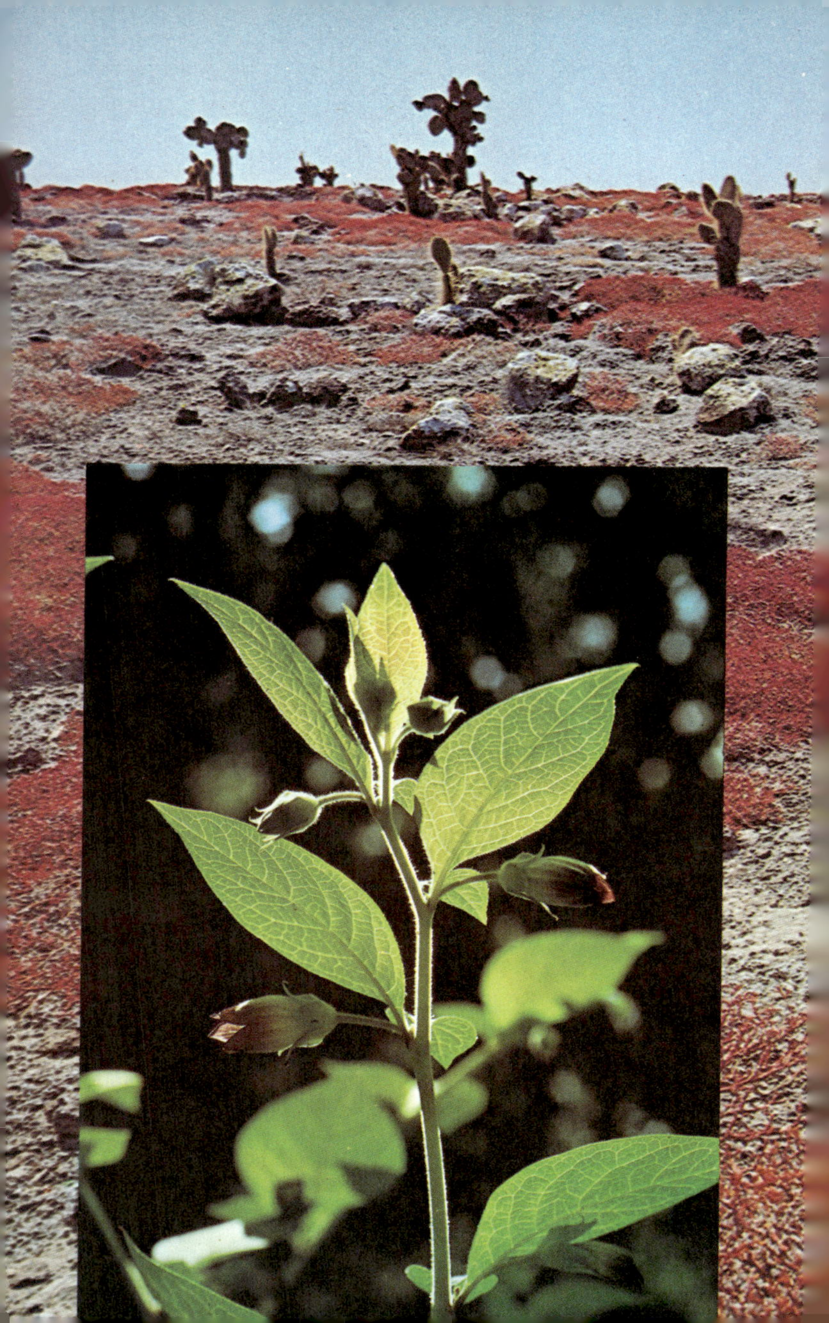

Plate 3 (Left) Deadly nightshade (*Atropa bella-donna*) taken against the light with a macro lens.

Plate 4 Las Plazas, Galapagos, in the dry season, dominated by the red succulent *Sesuvium edmonstonei*. Wide angle lens.

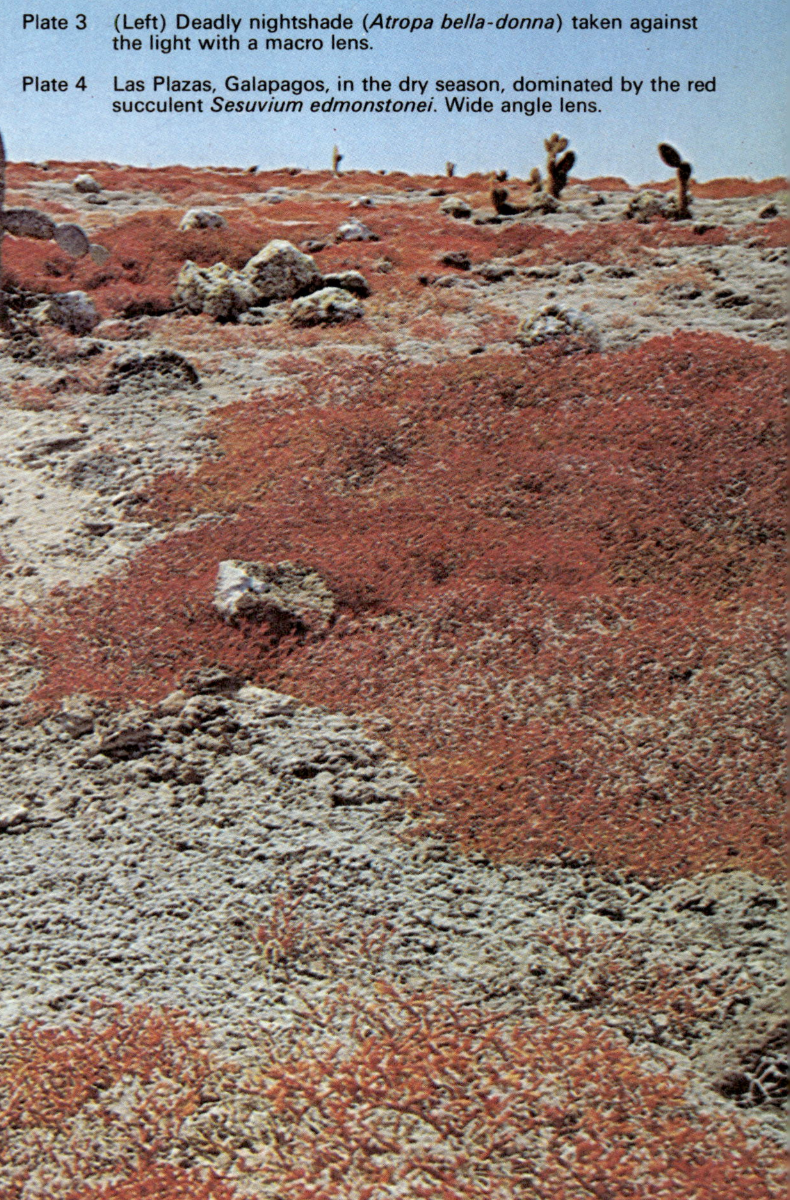

which experiences continuous summer light, the flowering season is condensed into a very short period, often a matter of days rather than weeks.

Climatic conditions on mountains are harsh and variable, and so the majority of alpines no longer depend on setting seed each year to propagate themselves. Since the variety of insects decreases with altitude, the majority of seed-producing alpines are wind instead of insect pollinated. Many cushion forms, however, are adapted to pollination by ants. Most alpines are perennial plants which, by utilizing food reserves from the previous season, can rapidly and simultaneously come into flower once the snow has melted. Some alpines, often prefixed with the name 'viviparous', reproduce by means of bulbils instead of by seeds.

Timing It is essential to determine beforehand the best time for seeing and photographing alpine flowers in a particular locality. Even then, there can be variations of a few weeks either side, owing to early or late seasons. The one advantage of mountain habitats is that spring begins low down and gradually progresses up the mountainside. If plants have finished flowering at one level, they may still be in prime conditions at a higher level.

Well known areas for alpine flowers in the European Alps are the Alpes Maritimes; the Dolomites; the Bernese Oberland, the Engadine and the regions around Wengen and Zermatt in Switzerland; and the Julian Alps in north Yugoslavia. Each area has its own range of alpine plants, including some endemics. The last two weeks in June is a good time to visit the central Swiss Alps; for the alpine meadows will not yet have been cut, and by climbing up to the snow-line, choice flowers such as the soldanellas will still be found. Farther east, the beginning of July is ideal; but even as late as the first week in August, alpine flowers can still be found on high passes at the snow line.

The Spanish Sierra Nevada is the highest mountain range in south-west Europe (3458m). Like Ben Lawers, it is composed mainly of mica schists. Above 2500m snow lies for nine months of the year, so that in this alpine zone (2500–3500m) the short flowering season is at its best in early August, whereas on the lower slopes of the Sierra (1000m) the flowering season begins early April.

Latitude also affects the time of flowering. In Scandinavia, alpines grow at much lower levels (including sea level) than farther south in the Alps. Distribution of alpines and their time of flowering is also affected by climatic variations, which often relate to aspect and topography. For instance, the vegetation is very dif-

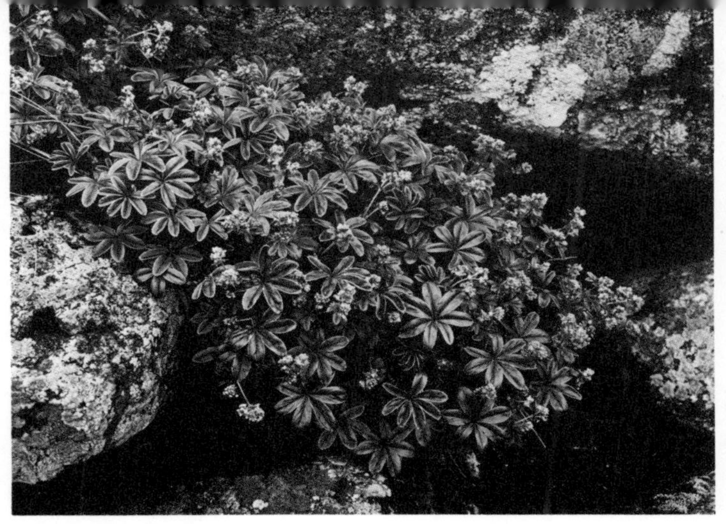

Fig. 2.2 A lady's mantle (*Alchemilla conjuncta*) in Angus, Scotland. Available diffuse lighting with a standard lens.

ferent on the north compared with the south side of the Pyrenees, which act as a climatic barrier. On the steeply sloping French side, the humid Atlantic air produces a heavy rainfall; whereas the series of parallel ridges and valleys on the Spanish side, are amongst the driest areas in Spain.

The westernmost limit of the Himalayan range in Kashmir, does not experience severe monsoons as it is a rain shadow area. Here, the best time for trekking and seeing the alpine flowers, is from late July to late September. In contrast, during June to mid-September the summer monsoons occur in the eastern Himalayas in Nepal and the mountains are then inaccessible. Treks in Nepal are best done from mid-September to the end of May, especially in the months of October/November and April/May.

Finding The books relating to mountain flowers which are listed in Appendix D, describe many well known regions for alpines; but even by knowing both the locality and the time of year, considerable effort must be put into searching in the field. The best way of getting to know where to look is to go out with an experienced field botanist, familiar with the area. Failing this, a pair of binoculars can be useful for scanning higher regions, as well as narrow ledges and areas across streams or boggy ground, to see if it is worth climbing higher or making a detour.

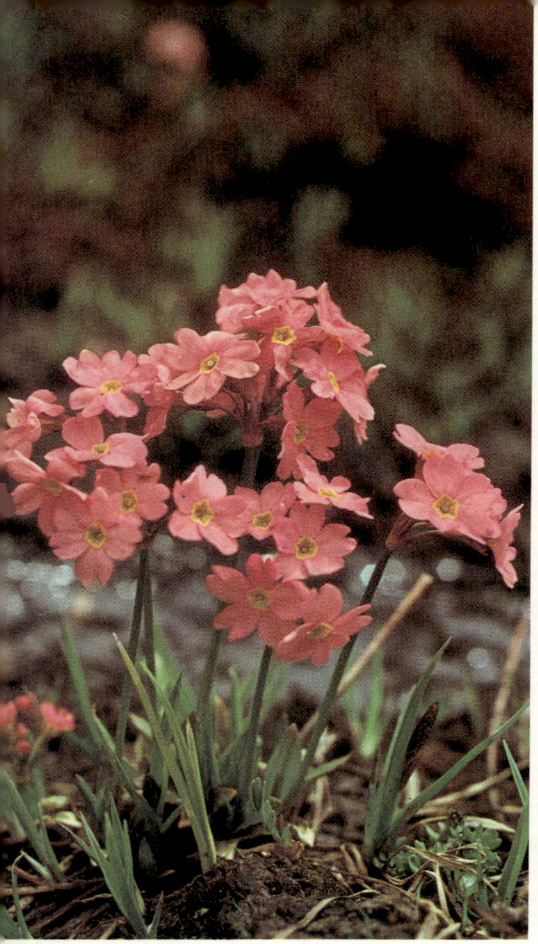

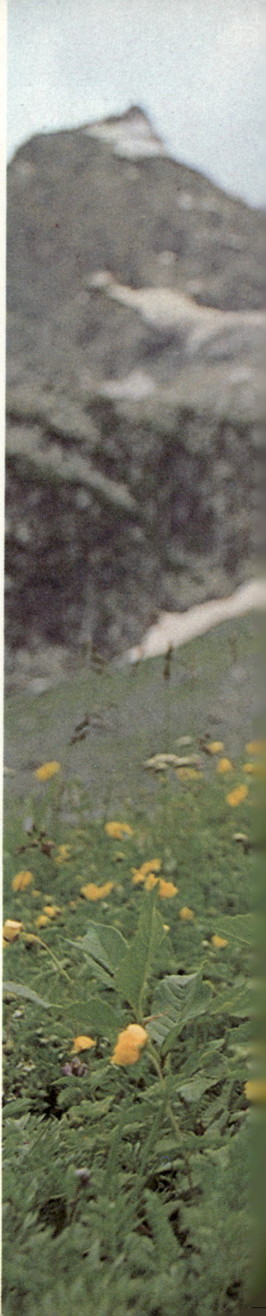

Plate 5 (Above) *Primula rosea* growing at 4000m in Kashmir. Available diffuse lighting, using a macro lens. ×1·5

Plate 6 Gaping salvia (*Salvia hians*) is endemic to Kashmir. Photographed at 3600m with a wide angle lens.

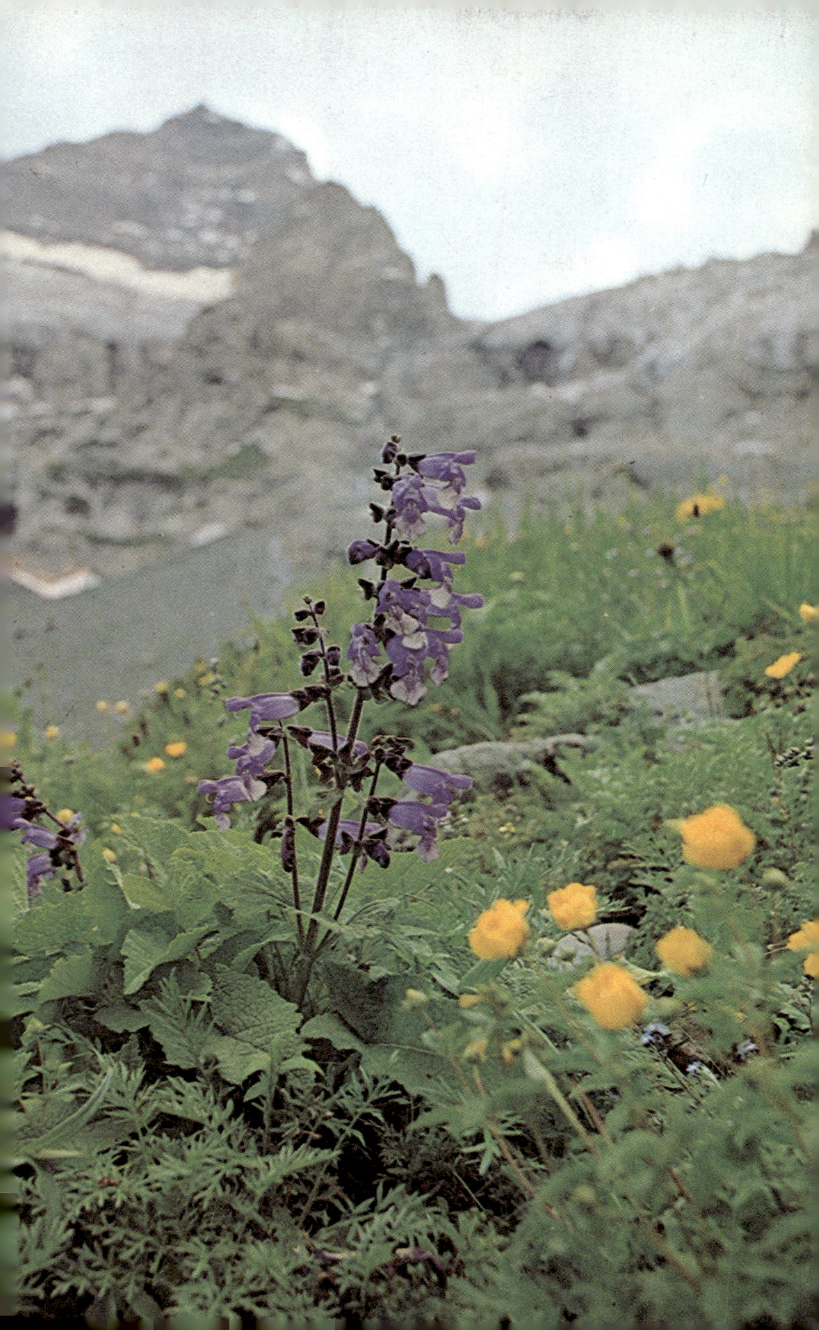

Recent snow-melt areas are always worth investigating for flowers which have finished flowering in warmer patches. The creeping primrose was reportedly a rare plant in Kashmir, and yet we found it repeatedly, when we climbed above 4200m and searched the bare ground in front of the retreating snow.

Rocky outcrops – especially if they include isolated pockets of limestone on an otherwise acidic mountainside – are also productive sites for alpines. Sheltered ledges where humus accumulates are often places with bright splashes of colour. Ledges which are inaccessible to goats and sheep invariably sport the choicest plants, but they usually prove equally inaccessible to the photographer. The effect of continuous grazing of alpine meadows becomes immediately apparent as soon as an area becomes fenced off. The legendary extensive flowery meadows of Gulmarg in Kashmir have gone. The fact that it sports the largest natural golf course in the world is of little consolation to the flower photographer!

Shade-loving plants, including ferns, will be found growing in deep crevices or hollows between boulders.

Mountainsides are not always dry. Water seeping down through the ground can collect in a hollow to form a flush of bog-loving plants – especially the bog moss, *Sphagnum*. The plants associated with these places are quite distinct from those of drier regions. Springs and streams are also well worth exploring for plants which like growing in wet ground.

Problems

The time and effort which must be spent in finding alpines makes their photography seem particularly rewarding, but once a choice specimen has been found, there are consistent climatic features which do not aid photography on mountains.

Ultra-violet The level of ultra-violet radiation is greatly increased with altitude, especially in areas of snow. Although these short wavelengths are invisible to the naked eye, they appear as a blue cast on colour photographs. Unless this effect is desired in a pictorial photograph, it is standard practice to keep an ultra-violet absorbing filter, such as a haze filter, permanently on the lens when photographing on mountains. This is not as essential for plant close-ups as for landscape and habitat pictures. Above 1500m a special ultra-violet filter is often used. An alternative technique is to use artificial light colour film with the 85 (salmon pink) conversion filter recommended for use in daylight.

Wind is the curse of alpine flower photographers. There are few situations which are wind free; even in apparently sheltered hollows, wind seems to appear from nowhere. Exposed places such as passes, summit ridges and peaks are persistently buffeted and typically the vegetation is wind-pruned.

At low altitudes, on windy days photography is best postponed; yet having climbed up a mountain, a photographer will want to make some attempt at getting a picture. Obvious ways of arresting moving plants are either to use a fast film and a fast shutter speed or to use flashlight. However, unless the background is close behind the plant, flashlight will produce a stark unlit 'nocturnal' background if it overrides the daylight. This is undesirable, as the aim when photographing mountain flowers is to show the flower in its ecological context.

A wind shield is rarely effective unless it encircles an arc of at least 240° around the plant and is made of a transparent material such as Perspex. It is also another item which has to be sweated up the mountainside.

If the wind is intermittent, relatively slow exposures may be possible with the camera on a tripod and by watching the plant, waiting until it becomes stationary.

Rain is another feature of the montane climate. All equipment should be carried in a waterproof bag. By no means all rucksacks are waterproof. Plastic sheeting is not ideal, since it sweats in the heat. An umbrella is useful for protecting a camera whilst photographing in a light shower, and if it has an inner reflective surface it can also be used for filling in shadows by reflecting available light or flashlight on to the subject. Rain spoils some flowers by washing out the pigments from their petals, so that they become spotted with white.

Heat may seem a strange heading to find in a chapter dealing with mountain flowers. However, during summer there are wide diurnal temperature fluctuations on mountains, which present special problems both to the photographer and the camper. Early in the morning and in the evening, when the sun is low in the sky, the temperature is cold enough to warrant wearing at least a couple of sweaters and an anorak. As the day progresses and if the sun shines and there is little wind, layers of redundant clothing can be peeled off. Sunburn is a real problem and bald-headed photographers will find a hat essential.

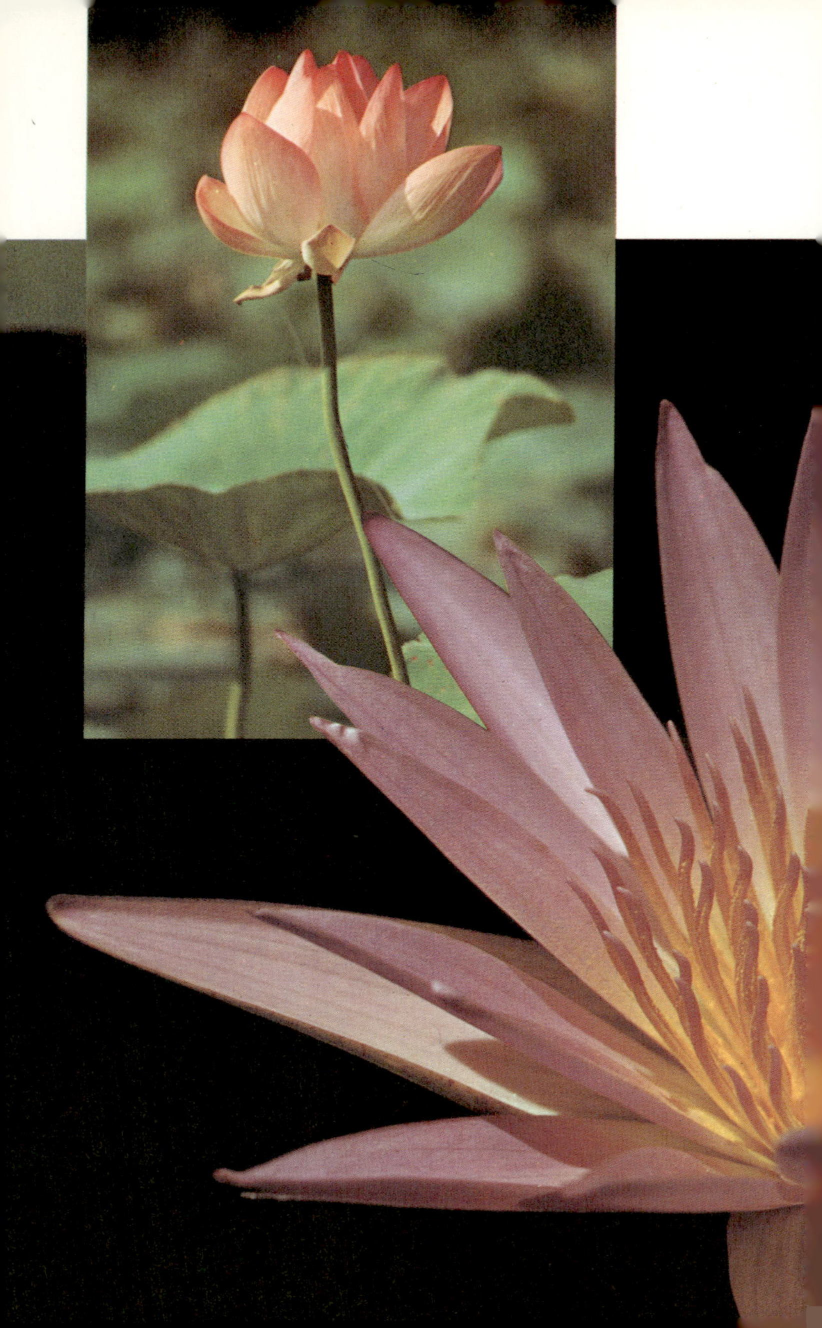

Plate 7 (Left) Lotus flower (*Nelumbo nucifer*) on Dal Lake, Kashmir. Photographed from a boat using a long focus lens.

Plate 8 A water lily on Lake Naivasha, Kenya. Taken in direct sunlight from a boat with a macro lens. ×1

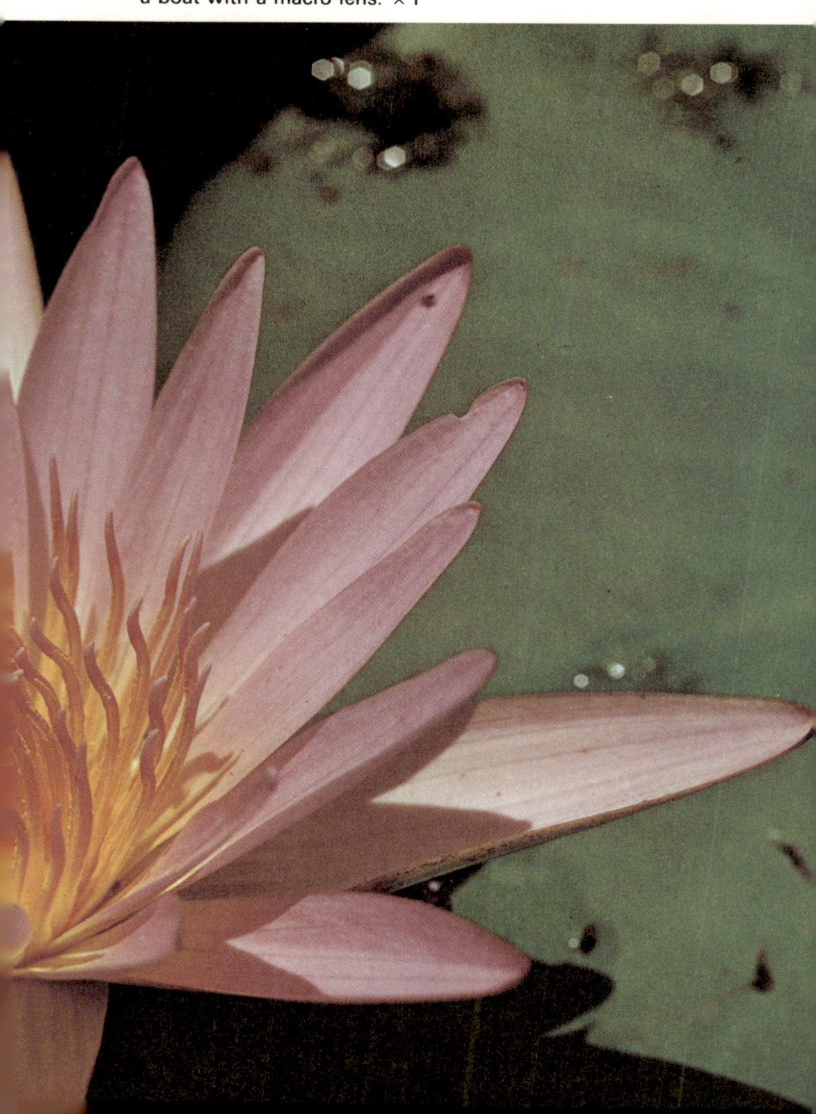

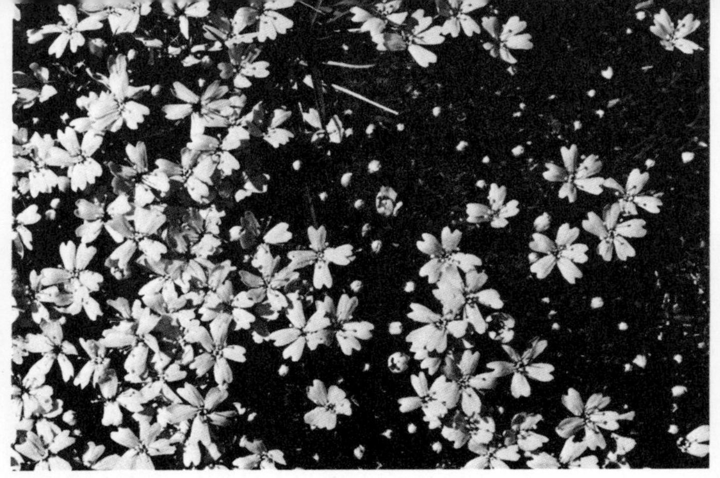

Fig. 2.3 Moss campion (*Silene acaulis*) carpet on Ben Lawers, Perthshire. Available lighting, with camera on reversed tripod head.

The temperature fluctuations present a problem of how to protect films which have to be carried around on mountains for several consecutive days. On a ten-day pony trek in Kashmir, I found the best way of keeping both unexposed and exposed films cool and dry, was to wrap them inside sleeping bags which were then packed inside a waterproof bag. In this way they were protected against the heat of the sun, rain and immersion in rivers as the pack ponies waded through with their sagging loads.

Photography

Mountain weather is notorious for rapid change. It is essential to carry a complete waterproof outfit. Proper mountain footwear is essential for safety and comfort. Carry all equipment in a rucksack, so that both hands can be kept free for climbing. A pocket compass and map should be standard equipment for any excursion into the mountains, which can suddenly become shrouded in mist and clouds. Leave details of your route with someone who can raise the alarm in case of an accident.

Pony-trekking is an ideal way of exploring mountain regions. Horseback often provides a better viewpoint than ground level for habitat pictures. For close-ups, however, it is obviously essential to dismount. Since horses invariably begin to feed as soon as they stop, it is a wise precaution not to stop too close to a choice alpine!

The techniques already described for close-up photography of plants in general can be applied to alpine flowers. A few additional techniques which are especially relevant to mountains are described below.

Erect plants are best photographed from the side, so as to show the flower or flower spike, stem and leaves. These plants are ideal for taking with a wide angle lens so as to include the mountain habitat behind (Plate 6 and Fig. 2.1). This technique can produce some very striking photographs, but it is not suitable for all alpine flowers. It is best used only for plants which have a bold shape or colour. The foreground plant should be sharply focused in preference to the distant mountains.

Creeping forms Many alpines, especially those growing in exposed situations, are compact plants which grow as rosettes, mats or cushions. Saxifrages often have a rosette of basal leaves surrounding the central flower stem. Mat-forming plants produce stems which branch in all directions as they creep over the ground. Cushion formers are very compact with a mass of short stems crowded together, and they often have enrolled leaves which helps to cut down loss of water by evaporation. These plants are well adapted to withstand the temperature extremes of day and night. Their resemblance to mosses is borne out by the prefix to some of their common names: moss campion (Fig. 2.3) and mossy cyphal.

Rosette plants with an erect flower stem will have to be photographed from the side in the same way as for taller plants. A ground spike is useful for photographing creeping plants with erect flowering spikes, such as dwarf willows, with a standard or a macro lens. Whenever a low angled viewpoint is used for photography, either a waist level viewfinder or a right-angle viewfinder attached to a fixed pentaprism, will save lying on the ground to focus the camera. Creeping and cushion-forming plants are often easier to take because they are less affected by the wind and, because they grow flat over the ground, the problem of the depth of field is not so acute. The best viewpoint for these plants is from directly overhead. Figure 2.3 was taken by supporting the camera on the reversed head of a tripod. Tripods can be used on uneven ground, providing the legs can be set and locked to any length. When there is no room on a narrow ledge to spread out all three tripod legs, an improvised camera support can be made by pushing the column against the vertical rock face and pulling one or two

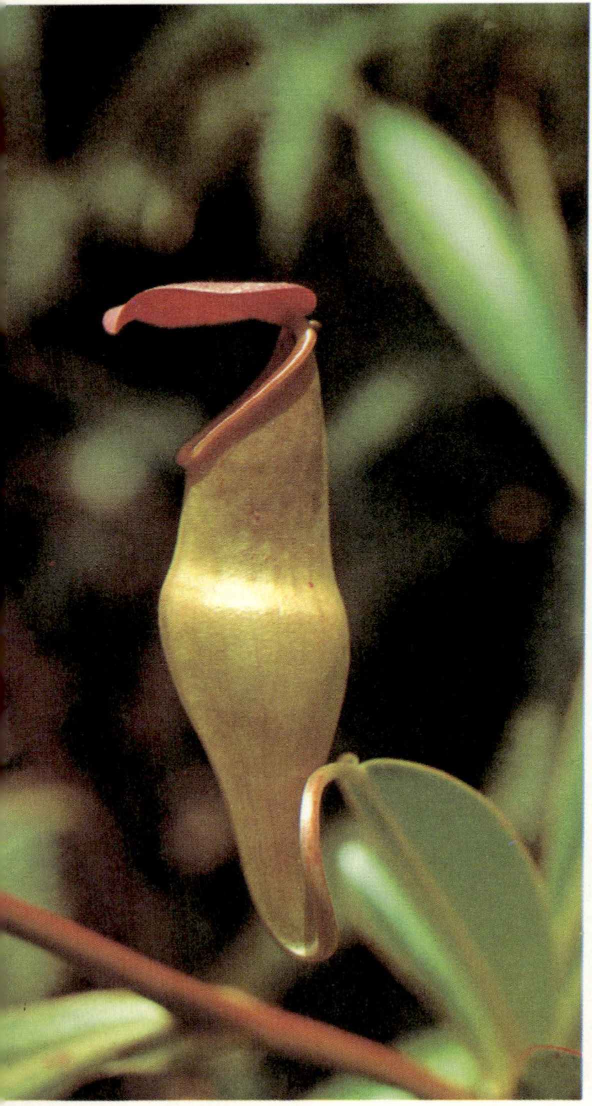

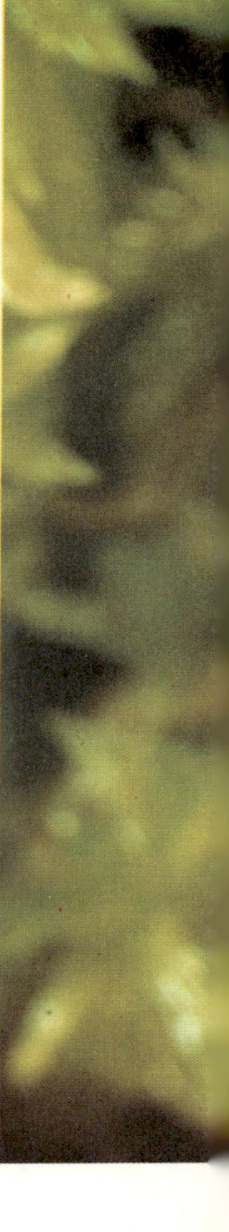

Plate 9 Insect-trapping pitcher plant (*Nepenthes pervillei*) is endemic to the Seychelles. Direct sunlight, with a macro lens. ×1

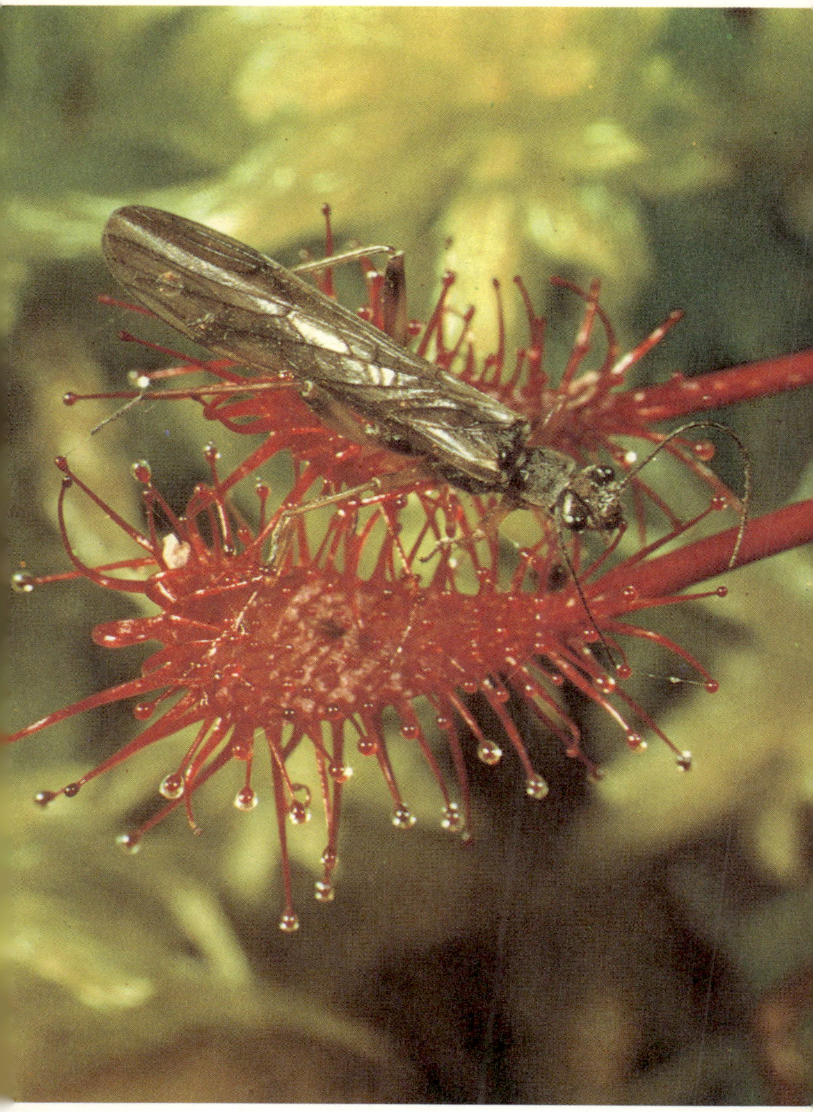

Plate 10 Insect trapped on sticky leaves of sundew (*Drosera intermedia*). Studio, with direct flash. Extension tubes. ×5

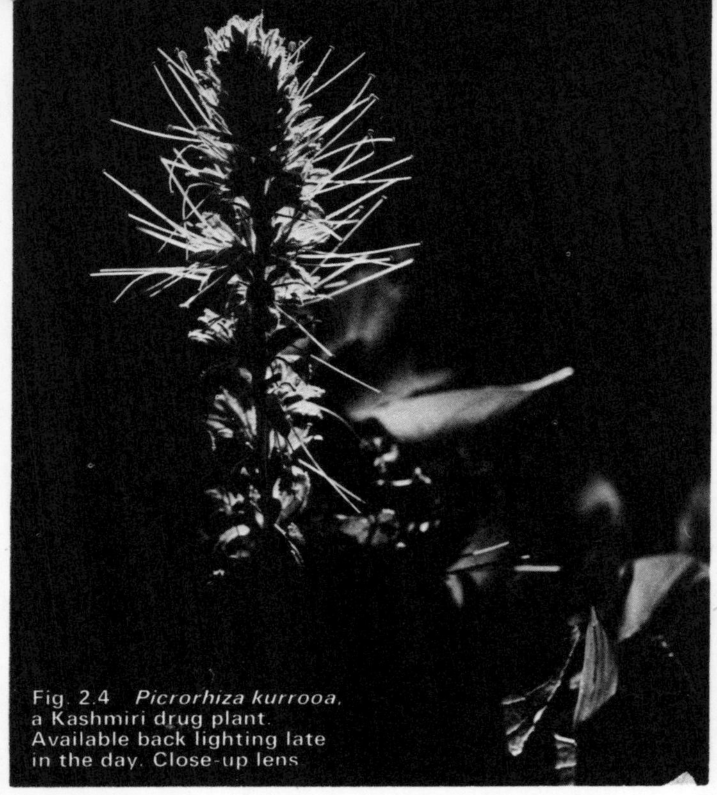
Fig. 2.4 *Picrorhiza kurrooa*, a Kashmiri drug plant. Available back lighting late in the day. Close-up lens

legs down so that they rest on the ground. The camera can then be used for taking an overhead view of a plant. If there is not room to stand alongside the plant on the ledge, it is possible to use the tripod in this way whilst sitting on a person's shoulders.

Shade plants grow in places where the sun never penetrates. Such places are the north facing walls (in the northern hemisphere), the underside of rocky overhangs, deep crevices and hollows. Ferns, in particular, are shade-loving plants, which tend to grow in dark situations where it is necessary to use either long exposures or flashlight. Like the crevice fauna of rocky shores, flashlight is essential for taking plants growing deep in crevices. The flash has to be used frontally, with the result that wet surfaces and water droplets in the background tend to be reproduced as distracting highlights.

White flowers are never easy to photograph. Direct sunlight produces a high contrast between pale petals and dark leaves both of which cannot be reproduced correctly on colour film. Even when using monochrome films under these conditions, the negatives will be very contrasty. Any subtle detail of venation pattern in white or pastel-coloured flowers becomes burnt out and lost by direct lighting. If possible, such flowers should be photographed by the soft diffuse lighting of overcast days. It is also possible to create diffuse lighting on a sunny day by shading the plants from the direct rays of the sun. A diffusing screen, such as a piece of muslin, held between the sun and the subject reduces the direct light to a soft illumination. An assistant may be needed to hold the diffuser in position.

Another method for monochrome films only, which is more practical for a photographer working on his own, is to use a green filter. This filter reduces the contrast between the white flowers and green leaves; the leaves appearing paler in the final print.

Blue flowers such as gentians, rarely come out on colour film as they appear to the eye. The reason is that both these and purple-blue flowers, reflect some red and infra-red in addition to the blue wavelengths. The human eye is not very sensitive to the red wavelengths so it sees the flowers as blue. Colour films, being more sensitive to the longer wavelengths, reproduce the flowers with a distinct pinkish or reddish cast. This discrepancy between the relative sensitivity of the eye and the film, can be reduced in a variety of ways, none of which is wholly satisfactory.

A pale blue colour correcting filter such as CC 10B or CC 20B (note these are *not* the same as the contrast filters used with monochrome films) can be used to cut down the reds and thereby accentuate the blues. Since these filters also affect the greens as well, they are best used only when the frame is completely filled with a blue flower. Although these filters are pale in colour, they cut out some wavelengths and so an exposure adjustment must be made. Photography by diffuse rather than direct light can help to bring out a truer blue rendering. Artificial light colour film used in daylight without a daylight correction filter results in an overall bluish cast to the pictures. So this is another way of increasing the intensity in a blue flower, but like the blue CC filters, this will also result in an overall blueness to the whole frame, including the rest of the vegetation.

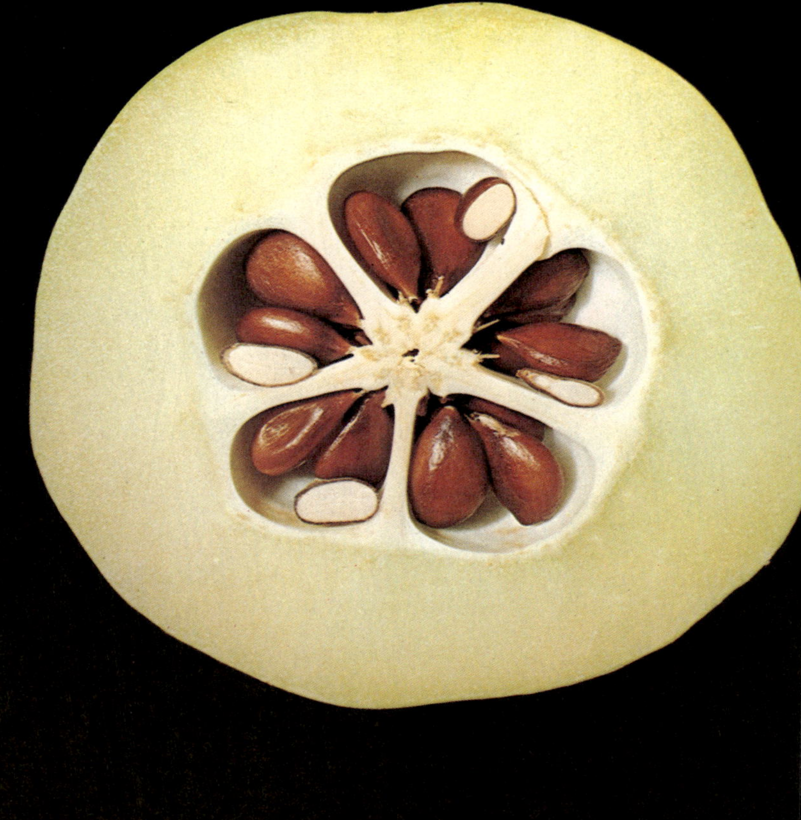

Plate 11 (Above) Transverse section of quince (*Cydonia oblonga*) fruit showing seeds in five-part ovary. Studio, with direct flashlight. Extension tubes. ×1·5

Plate 12 Fruit of *Rosa rugosa typica* taken in diffuse available light with a macro lens. ×1

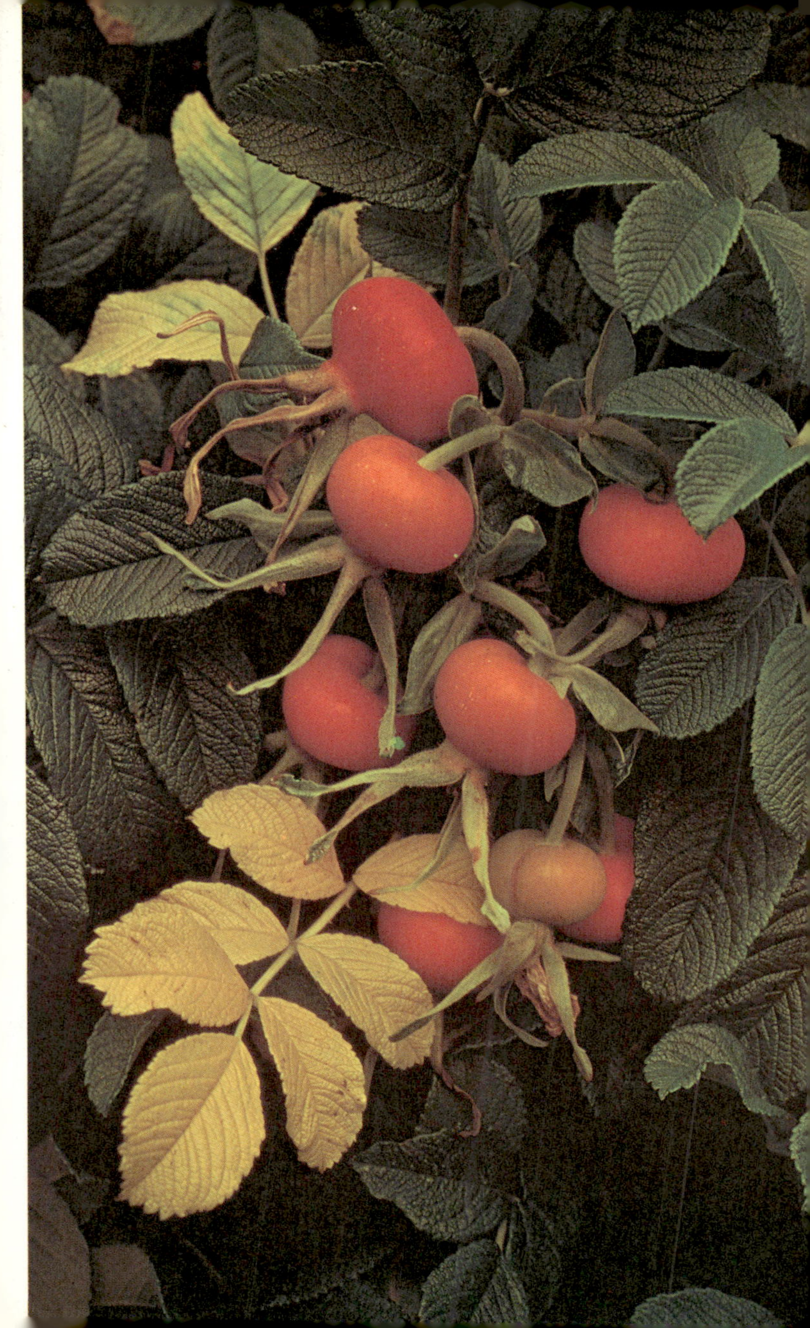

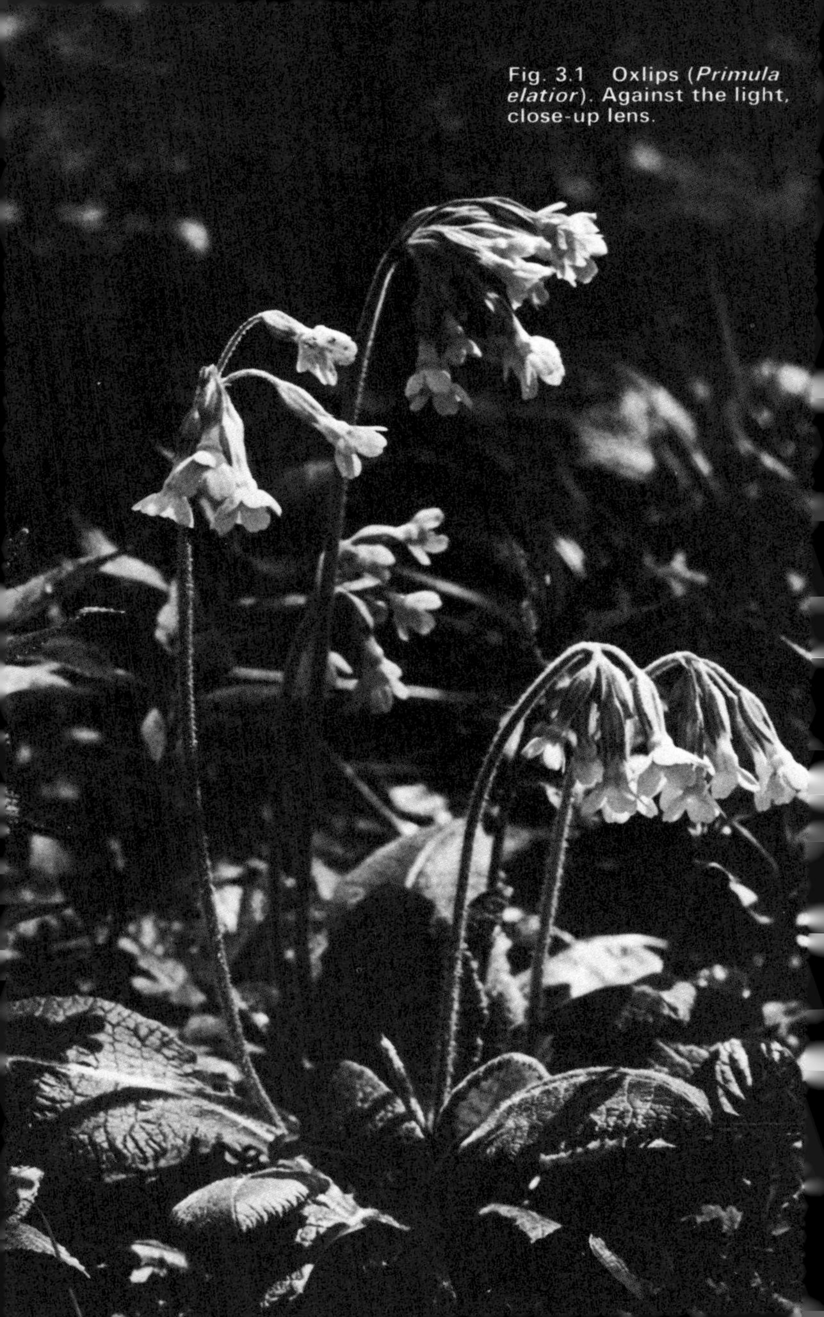

Fig. 3.1 Oxlips (*Primula elatior*). Against the light, close-up lens.

Trees and shrubs in forests and woodlands protect the ground flora from exposure, but they also cast shade over the ground for all or part of the year. The lack of light inside woodlands and forests is therefore much more of a problem to the photographer than wind.

Photographic studies of woodland flowers can be used for recording the flowers which appear month by month in a particular wood or forest, or for comparing the ground flora of different woodland types.

On the ground

In deciduous woodlands, light-demanding plants flower in the spring before the trees have leafed out. Snowdrops are one of the first spring flowers to form extensive carpets (Fig. 1.2) in some woodlands. Slightly later, carpets of primroses, wood anemones and bluebells are a more familiar sight. A wide angle lens is useful for showing the habitat and massed effect of these woodland flowers. However, if the camera is tilted upwards, it will produce distorted images of the trees, showing them leaning in towards the centre of the frame. If the trees are old gnarled oaks or beeches, the distortion will be barely discernible, but if they are trees with straight boles, it will be unacceptable. A special kind of wide angle lens known as a perspective correcting (PC) lens, normally used for architectural photography, is ideal for photographing trees. By off-centring the lens, it corrects the perspective distortion due to tilting the camera.

The flowers of the carpet formers, generally contrast well with the colour of the leaf litter and the surrounding vegetation and so they stand out clearly on colour film. Although a wide angle lens can be used to show a plant in context with its habitat (Fig. 3.2), to illustrate the structure of the plants and especially the flowers themselves, it is necessary to get in closer with either a macro lens or a standard lens and extension tubes (Fig. 3.4). Once again, a low level camera support, such as a ground spike, is ideal for the smaller components of the ground flora.

When deciduous forest trees have lost their leaves and also at any time of the year where there is a gap in the canopy, sun streams on to the forest floor casting a mosaic of light and shade. Such a contrast is beyond the latitude of colour films and so better woodland photographs will be taken in the diffuse lighting of slightly

Plate 13 (Below) Fruit of wayfaring tree (*Viburnum lantana*) taken in direct sunlight, with a macro lens. ×2

Plate 14 Creeping thistle (*Cirsium arvense*) dispersing seeds. Taken against the light with extension tube. ×1·5

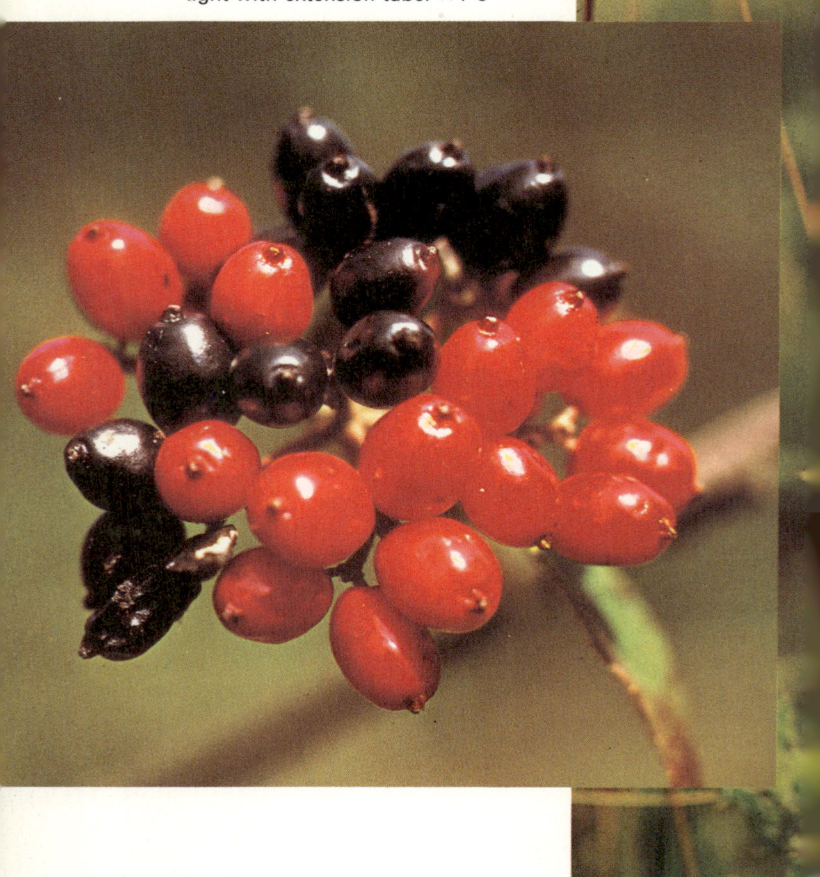

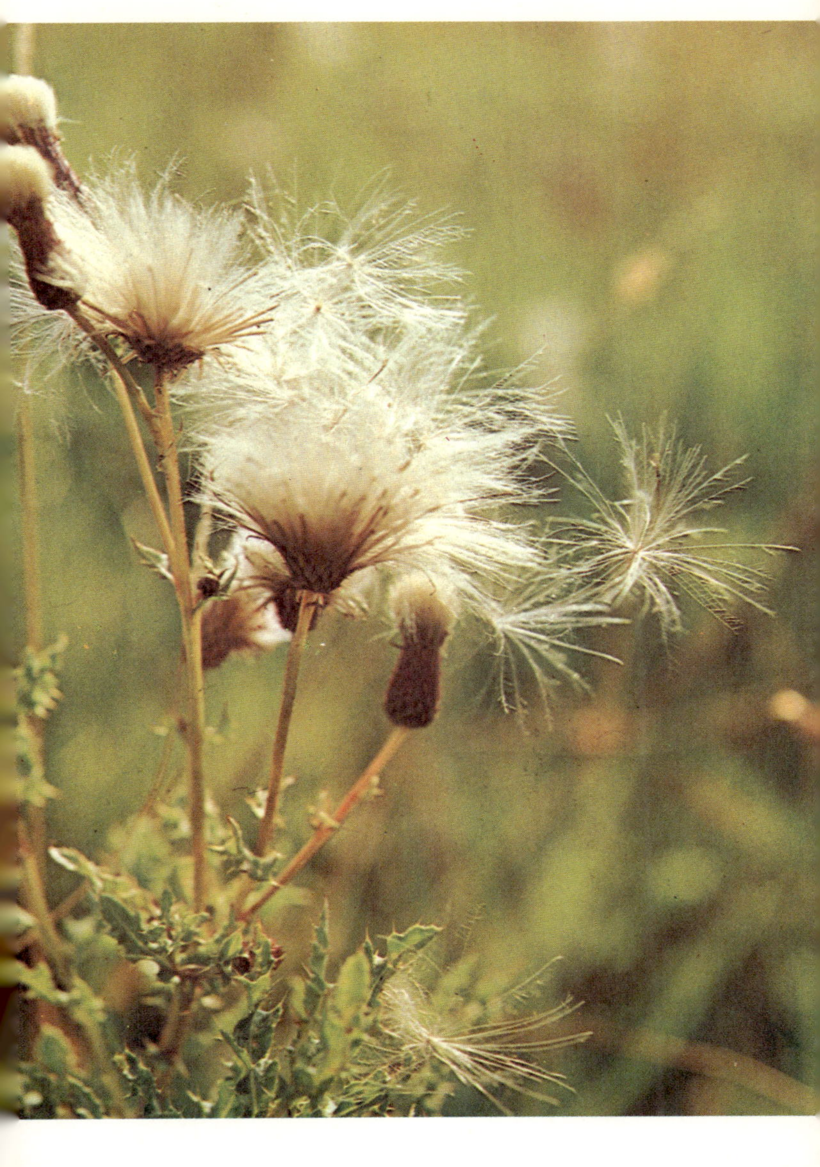

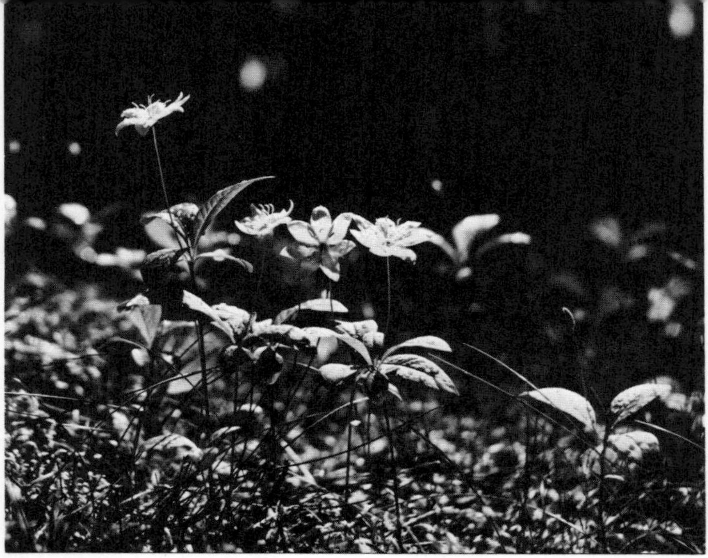

Fig. 3.2 Chickweed wintergreen (*Trientalis europaea*) in a Scottish pinewood spotlit by a shaft of sunlight. Wide angle lens.

Fig. 3.3 Honeysuckle (*Lonicera periclymenum*) spotlit by evening sun. Close-up lens.

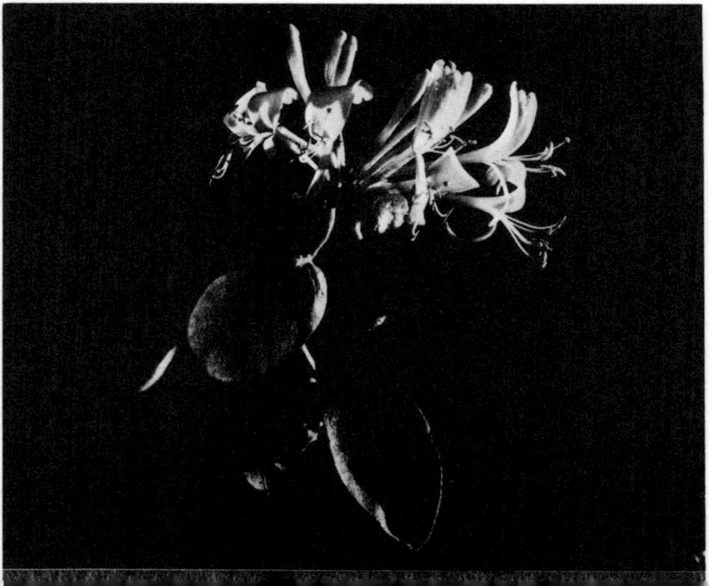

overcast days. Providing no wind is blowing, long exposures can be used with the camera on a tripod, but problems of reciprocity failure arise when using long exposures with colour film, as mentioned on page 21. For white and pale-coloured flowers, soft diffuse lighting is preferable to either direct sunlight or direct flashlight (page 23). A shaft of sunlight shining directly on the back of a single plant, or a compact group, can produce a dramatic spotlighting effect which is particularly successful for erect woodland flowers (Fig. 3.2). When sunlight shines through a flat leafy branch close beside a flower, it can throw an unnatural colour cast on to the plant, which may not be apparent to the naked eye, but will be discernible on colour film. Transillumination through green spring leaves or brown autumnal leaves is like shining a light through coloured cellophane.

In forest clearings and alongside woodland rides, a series of flowers appear throughout spring and summer. In these more open areas, lighting is less of a problem, but wind is more of one.

Flowers which live parasitically on the roots of other plants and also some orchids which form an underground root association with a fungus (Fig. 3.4), are not dependent on sunlight for building up their food supply. These flowers often grow in the darkest regions where they face least competition from green plants, so they may have to be taken on colour film with flashlight. When flashlight is used indirectly by bouncing it off a reflective surface, it will give softer-edged shadows than if it is used directly. In a dark wood, especially late in the evening, a torch strapped on to a flash will aid critical focusing and will also indicate where the light and shadows will fall.

The flora associated with evergreen pinewoods is quite distinct from deciduous woodlands, and varies in different parts of Britain. In southern England, where most pinewoods develop on heathland areas, bilberry and heather dominate the ground flora; whereas in Scottish pinewoods, chickweed wintergreen (Fig. 3.2), wintergreens and several orchids (creeping lady's tresses, coral root and lesser twayblade) occur.

Natural scale Leaves, coniferous needles, cones or acorns lying on the forest floor provide a useful comparative scale for close-up flower photographs. Usually they will appear somewhere in the field of view as in Fig. 3.4, but if they are not visible, it is quite legitimate to introduce a few pine needles or a beech leaf into the picture. Make sure, however, they do not dominate the photograph and thereby divert attention away from the flower itself.

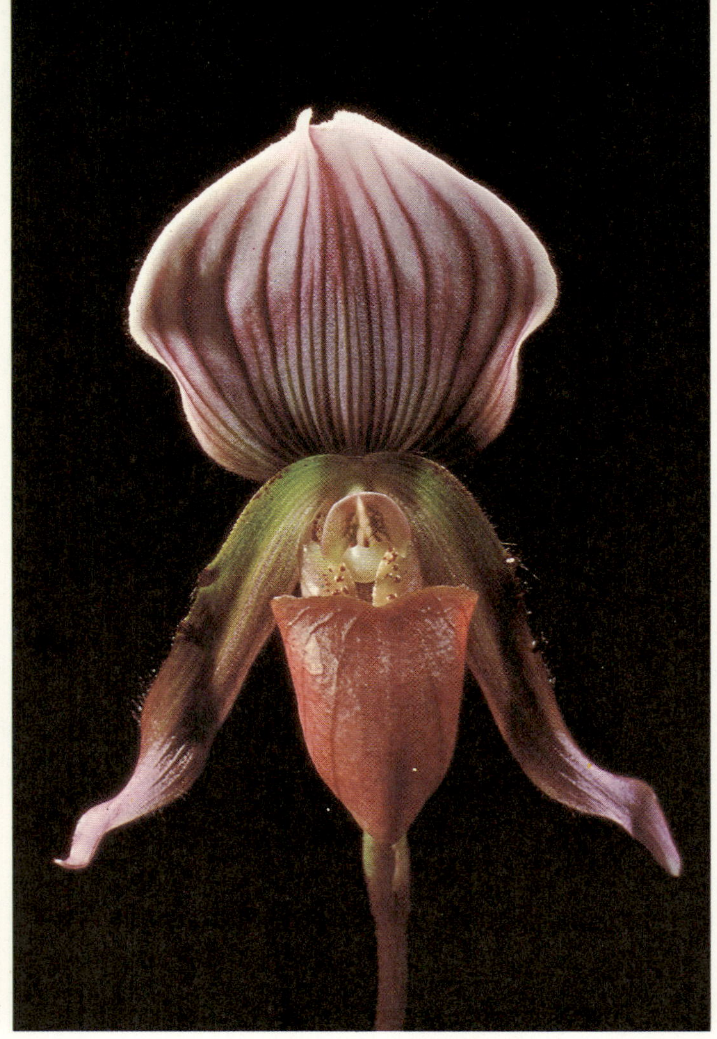

Plate 15 A cultivated slipper orchid. Studio, with dual source oblique flash. Extension tubes. $\times 2$

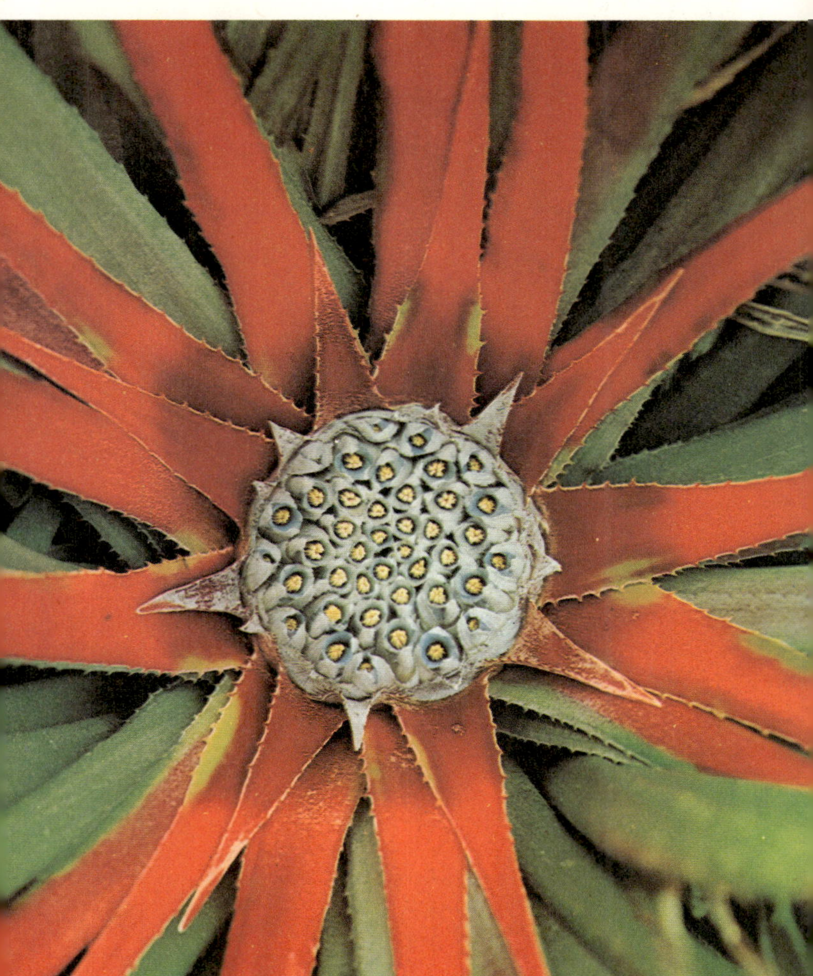

Plate 16 A Chilean bromeliad (*Fascicularia bicolor*) growing in a Cornish garden. Available diffuse lighting, using a close-up lens.

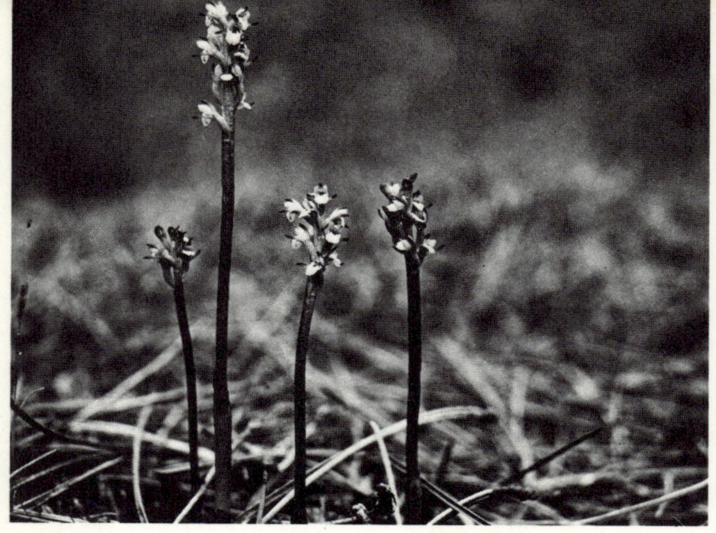

Fig. 3.4 Coralroot orchids (*Corallorhiza trifida*) in a Scottish pinewood. Available diffuse lighting with extension tubes. Pine needles provide natural scale. ×1

On trees

Plants which grow on trees do so to avoid competition at ground level, to receive more light or to feed from the tree itself. No matter for what reason plants grow on trees, they present the same problems for photography. Climbing plants, such as honeysuckle, grow up from ground level and use the trunk as a means of support. Plants which grow on trees without having any connection with the ground and without feeding on the tree itself, are known as epiphytes. In Britain, the commonest epiphytes are the mosses and lichens which grow on trees in the wetter, west part of the country. In tropical rain forests, where the humidity is high and the overhead canopy is dense, many flowering plants such as orchids and bromeliads (Fig. 3.5) live as tree epiphytes. Parasites also grow on trees, unattached to the ground, but unlike epiphytes, they feed off the trees.

A long focus lens can be useful for photographing climbers, epiphytes or parasites from ground level, but the underside of a plant does not make an ideal viewpoint. A better perspective may be gained by climbing up a neighbouring tree or a stepladder. Unless a fast film is used, the camera will have to be supported by some method. A tripod cannot be used in a conventional way up

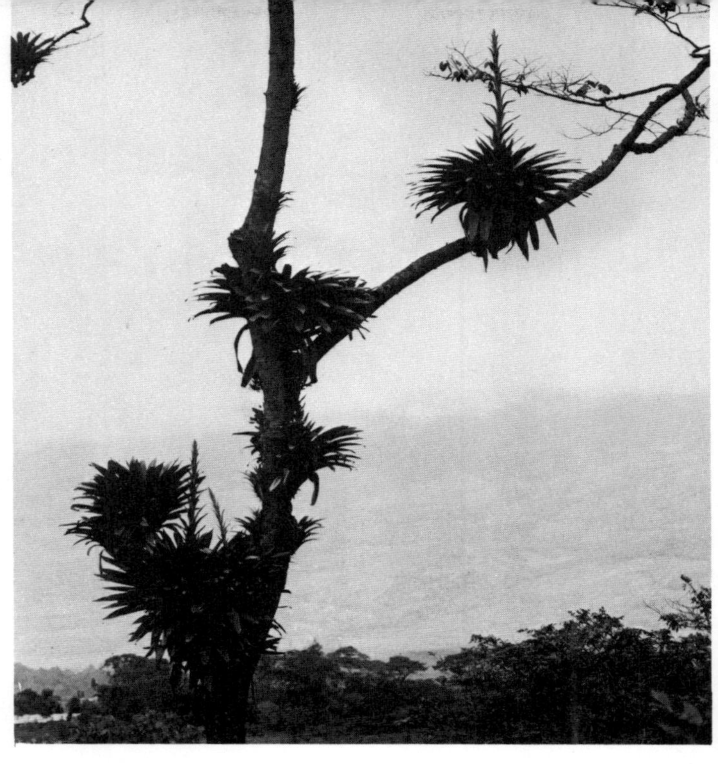

Fig. 3.5 Epiphytic bromeliads growing in Colombia, South America. Available lighting and long focus lens.

a tree, but it can be used by supporting the legs at right angles to the trunk, in a way similar to that described for photographing alpine flowers on a narrow ledge on page 41. An alternative camera support is a tree clamp, which theoretically should be ideal for photographing flowers growing on trees. In practice, there is rarely a convenient branch in quite the right place.

If the light is poor and parts of the plants are moving, flashlight will have to be used. In which case, because of the rapid fall off in the flashlight, it is essential to work at close range. As well as the flowers of climbers and epiphytes, the organs used for climbing or attachment to the tree – the suckers, hooks or tendrils – make interesting photographic subjects.

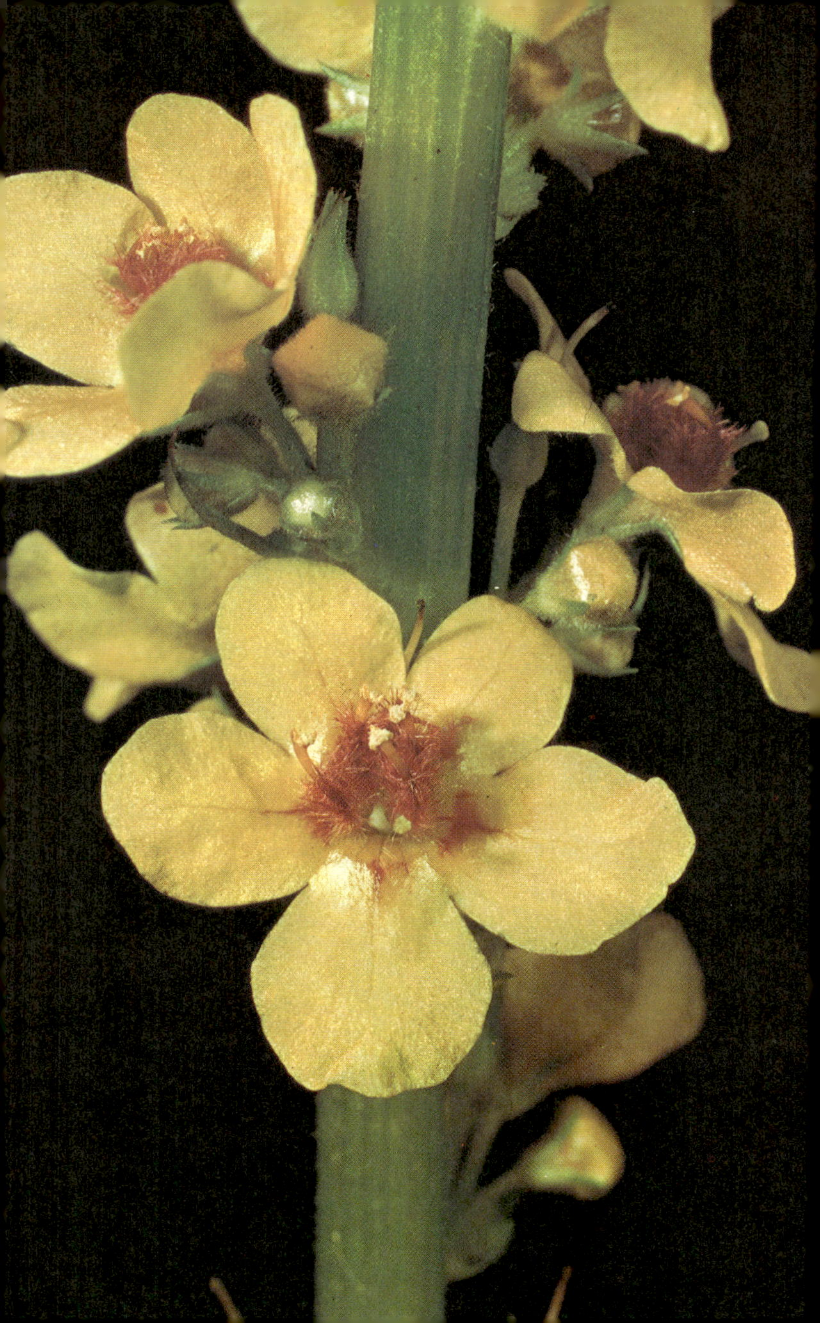

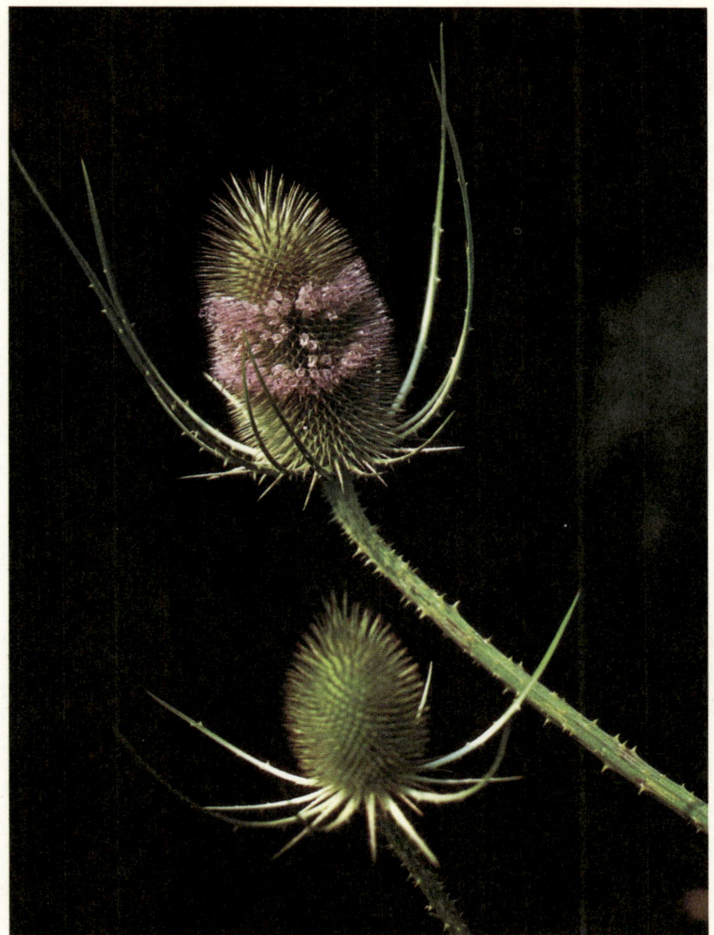

Plate 17 (Left) Dark mullein (*Verbascum nigrum*). Studio, dual source oblique flash. Extension tubes. ×3

Plate 18 Teasel flowers (*Dipsacus fullonum*) photographed in direct sunlight against a background in shadow.

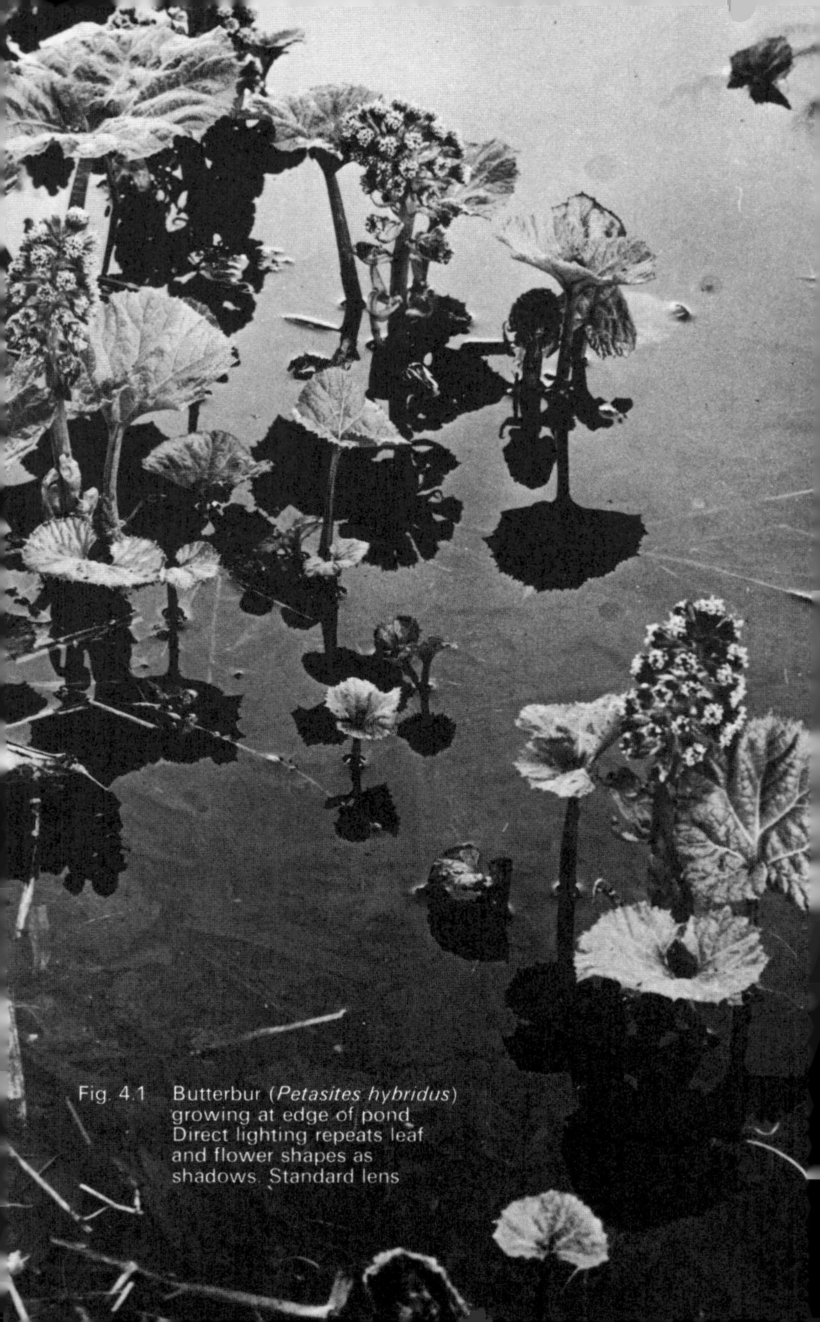

Fig. 4.1 Butterbur (*Petasites hybridus*) growing at edge of pond. Direct lighting repeats leaf and flower shapes as shadows. Standard lens

Plants which grow in water-logged and true aquatic habitats, present distinct problems for photography; but many beautiful as well as interesting plants are confined to wetlands. During the dry season, when the water level is low, many marshes and swamps can be explored on foot. Pond, canal and riverside banks are also accessible for photography, but a boat is essential for photographing plants growing in large lakes.

From land

Although the flora of swamps, marshes, fens and bogs is quite distinct in different parts of the world, the same techniques for photography can be applied anywhere.

Swamps It is wise to determine if there are any local hazards, dangerous animals or water-borne diseases before wading out into a swamp. Some of the gear worn by fly fishermen is ideal for swamp photography, especially waders and a waterproof pouch. Depending on the temperature, wear gum-boots or waders with warm clothing or plimsolls with a bathing costume. The problem with the latter combination is that there are no convenient pockets for carrying accessories! When working in the tropics, it is inadvisable to wade into freshwater with bare legs, not so much because of blood-sucking leeches, as because of the risk of infection by parasites and diseases such as bilharzia.

When exploring new ground, it is a wise precaution to leave the camera on a dry patch while making a preliminary reccé to determine the hazards and depth of water. If a local person cannot be found to act as a guide, use a stick to prod the bottom. Even when a safe route has been found, it is sensible to return with the minimum of equipment. Do not make the mistake I made wading into a mangrove swamp in the Galapagos, carrying a tripod and a rucksack full of equipment. After setting up the tripod, I realized there was nowhere to put down the rucksack and so I had to call someone over to extract a camera for me.

Mangrove swamps are typical of tropical brackish waters. Photographically, they are comparable with the alder carr which develops on temperate fenland areas which are not grazed or cut; in both habitats a mass of intertwining woody stems form (and also aerial roots in the case of mangroves) which can make penetration

Plate 19 (Below) Crocuses taken on a macro lens with direct flashlight to arrest movement and increase depth of field. ×2·5

Plate 20 Detail of musk thistle (*Carduus nutans*) head showing individual florets. Studio, with dual source oblique flash. Macro lens. ×3

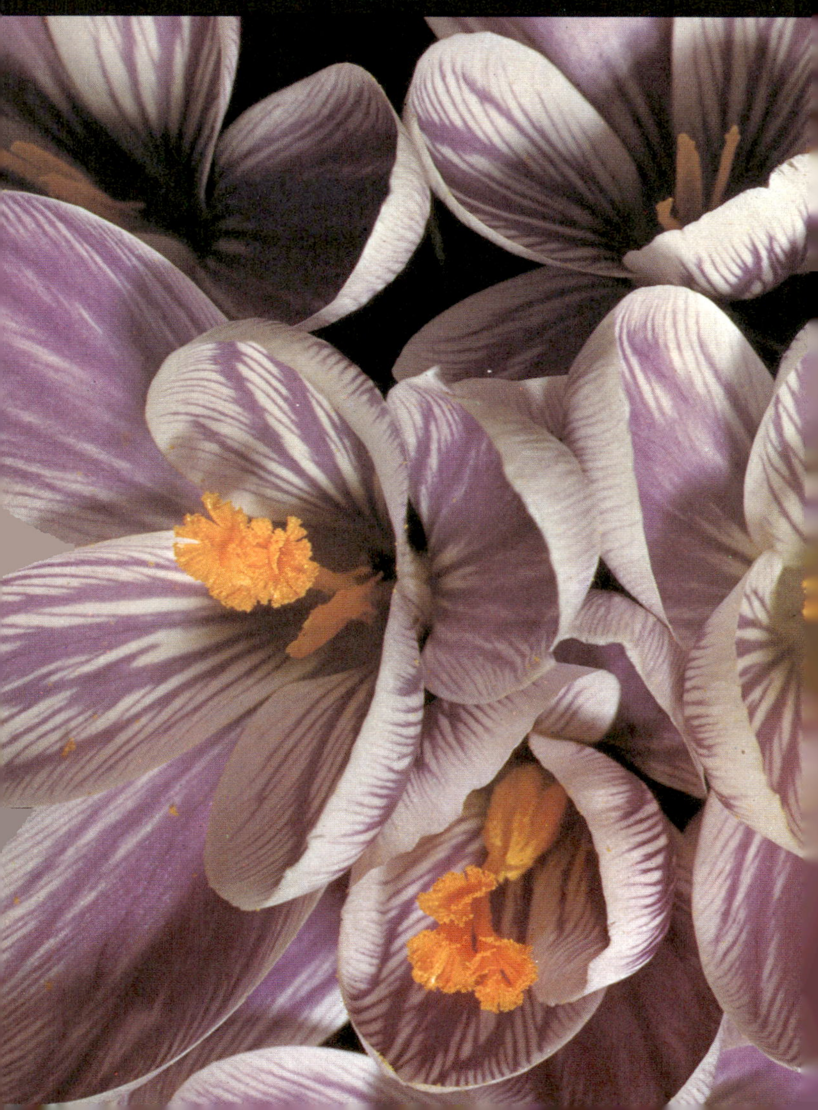

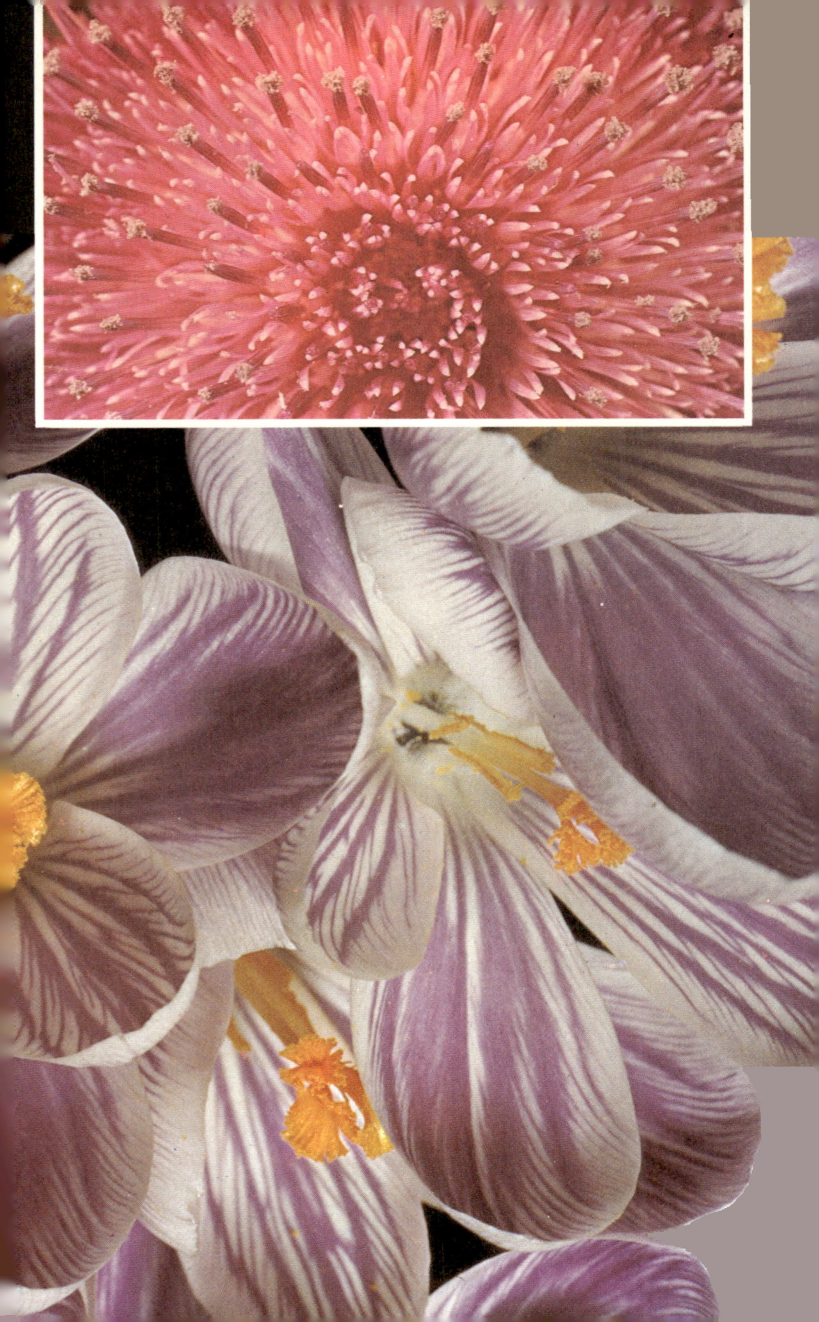

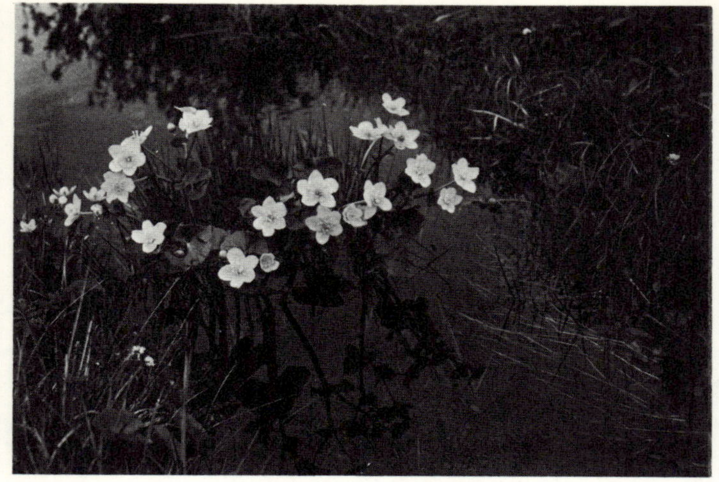

Fig. 4.2 Marsh marigolds (*Caltha palustris*) with reflections. Available lighting.

difficult. In summer, the light level inside swamps and carrs is low, and so a tripod is essential for taking any general habitat pictures, while a flashlight is ideal for close-up pictures. Be careful not to immerse the end of the flash lead in the water, and, if possible, avoid changing lenses.

Marshes, fens and bogs In contrast to fens, which have peaty (organic) soils, marshes develop on inorganic soils which may be silt or clay. The open stretches of these habitats are generally more accessible and therefore easier for photography, than swamps. Rushes are typical marshland plants, and whenever they are seen growing, it is a sure indication that the ground is wet. Typically, fenland soil is alkaline, but it can also be neutral or even slightly acidic. As with marshes, fens have their own flora, but some species can be found in both habitats.

Boglands are acidic peaty wetlands which have a distinct flora dominated by the bog mosses (*Sphagnum* spp.). The fauna which is also interesting, is unfortunately dominated by biting midges! Cotton grass is a widespread plant of boggy regions and its fluffy white seed heads are a sure sign that the ground is water-logged. Several different kinds of insectivorous plants grow in boglands.

They capture insects to gain an additional supply of nitrogen, which is essential to plant growth. The long-leaved sundew (Plate 10) is one of three kinds of sundews found in Britain, which trap insects in the sticky fluid secreted by long glandular hairs on their leaves. Butterwort captures small insects on its sticky basal leaves, while bladderwort traps small aquatic crustaceans in its underwater bladders (Fig. 4.5).

Critical close-up work in wetlands inevitably involves crouching or kneeling on soggy ground. A plastic mac or an old fertilizer sack makes a lightweight, waterproof mat, both for kneeling and for resting a gadget bag. The survival blanket described on page 21, can also be used for this purpose. Plants which creep over the bog surface are best photographed from overhead. A tripod or a ground spike can be used on the surface of some bogs, providing the legs or spike are pushed down into the moss and, to avoid any chance of camera shake, the delayed action mechanism is used. Since the bog may consist of a great mat of moss floating on top of water, any movement made during the exposure is liable to shake the surface for up to several metres around. Avoid repeatedly trampling over the same part of the bog surface, since it is easily destroyed and plants damaged.

Some boglands develop a system of raised hummocks and pools. As the tops of the hummocks grow up above the water level they dry out, the bog moss dies and eventually the top of the hummock erodes away. These pools, and indeed any area of water, can provide a simple uncluttered background for photographing bog plants in close-up.

Waterside margins Both floating and emergent plants growing close to the banks of ponds, canals or streams can be photographed using a standard or a macro lens. Emergent plants growing some distance from the bank may require a long focus lens to concentrate attention on one particular flower or plant. Figure 4.3 was taken in this way, and the dense covering of duckweed provided a uniform pale background in contrast to the silhouetted leaves. A tow path alongside a canal provides a good viewpoint for larger plants; whereas details of small plants will be seen only by wading in at the water's edge. Having ruined one camera by immersing it, I attach the camera to the tripod in ponds and canals only once I am confident that the legs are firmly pressed into the substrate. Any disturbance of the bottom will stir up the mud and debris, but this may help to provide a better contrast to floating leaves than dark clear water.

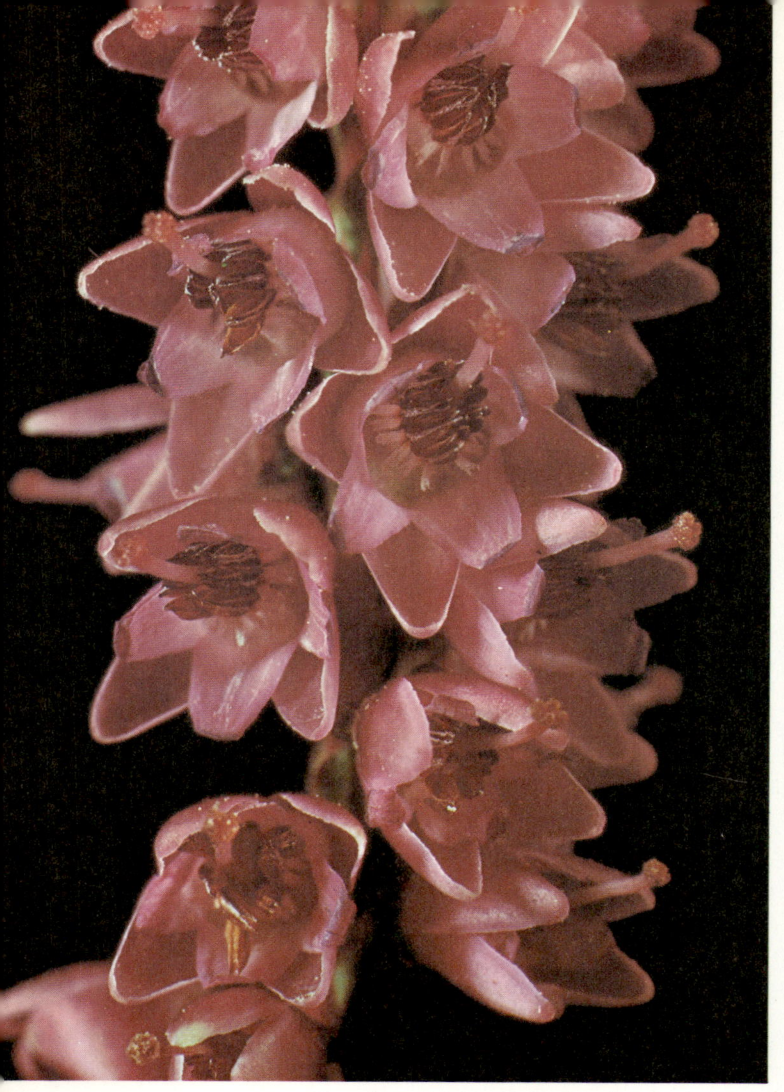

Plate 21 Heather (*Calluna vulgaris*) in studio, with dual source oblique flash and bellows. ×10 M

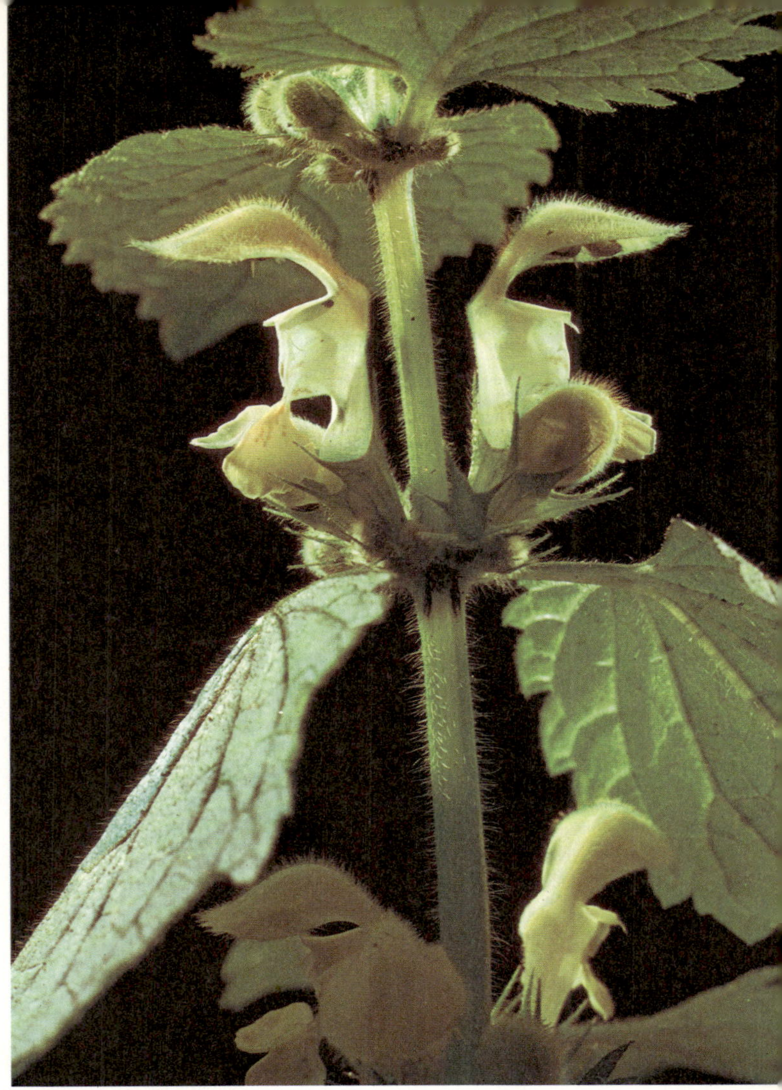

Plate 22 Detail of white dead-nettle (*Lamium album*). Studio, dual source oblique lighting from behind. Bellows. ×2

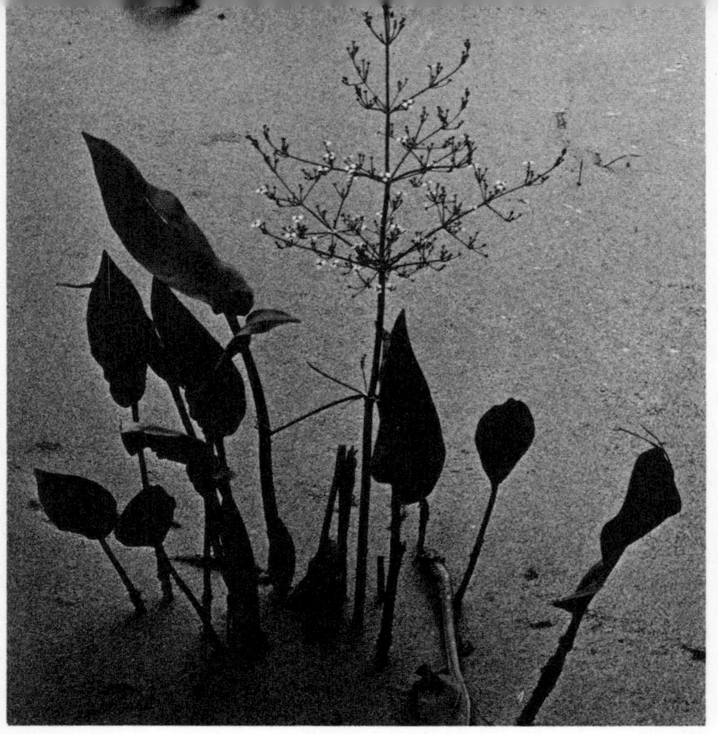

Fig. 4.3 Water plantain (*Alisma plantago-aquatica*) taken against the light. Silhouetted leaves isolated by uniform carpet of duckweed. Long focus lens.

Surface reflections Whenever photographs are taken looking down on to water of floating plants on the surface or of submerged plants underwater, there is always the possibility that reflections of clouds, trees, the camera or even of the photographer, will ruin the picture. When using an SLR camera, the extent of these reflections can be seen by stopping the lens down to the preselected aperture. If they are too distracting, either use a polarizing filter or make a return visit at a different time of day or on an overcast day. A polarizing filter will reduce surface reflections only when it is used at a critical angle (37°) to the water. The $1^1/_2$ stops exposure increase required with this filter effectively reduces the film speed, which can be a serious limitation when using a slow speed colour film.

Shiny leaves A polarizing filter can also be used to reduce distracting reflections on floating leaves with a thick waxy cuticle. An easier solution may be to adjust the camera angle relative to the sun.

From boats

To be paddled amongst a carpet of water lilies must surely be one of the most idyllic ways of photographing flowers. When I am sweating my way up a mountainside, I think back to the days spent on Lake Naivasha in Kenya and Lakes Dal and Anchar in Kashmir, doing just that.

Early in the morning the water lily flowers are tight buds. As the day warms up the flowers open and by the evening they have closed again. Narrow flat-bottomed boats called shikars are used for transport on Dal and Anchar Lakes. The skilful paddlers soon learnt to stop paddling before the boat reached a plant I wanted to photograph, so that we did not drift past it. Emergent flowers such as the lotus lily (Plate 7) can be photographed by sitting down and using a long focus lens. But floating flowers such as the water lily (Plate 8) as well as floating leaves need a higher viewpoint with the boat close beside them. When working in a small boat care must be taken to make sure it is well trimmed before gently leaning over the side. It is also advisable to put all gear in a waterproof bag or case, since a puddle of water invariably collects in the bottom of boats.

Even when moored or anchored, boats are never stationary, so that a tripod is of little use. A boat can be steadied and kept in position by a passenger holding on to rooted weeds or a post. However, any slight movement by a fellow passenger or waves set up by a passing boat, will immediately set it rocking. It is therefore advisable to use fairly fast shutter speeds – certainly faster than is normal practice for hand-holding on land.

In the studio

Small floating plants, as well as submerged plants, can be photographed more easily and critically in an aquarium, indoors.

Collection Floating plants can be collected by scooping them up into a jar or a bucket or by fishing with a net. Rooted plants may have to be carefully pulled up by hand. To prevent them drying out and dying, they should be transferred immediately to a bucket or jar with some water.

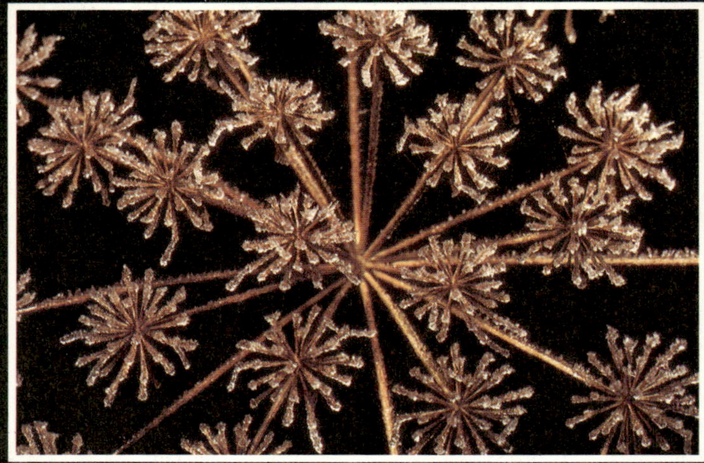

Plate 23 (Above) Hoar frost on dried hogweed head (*Heracleum sphondylium*). Direct flashlight used to isolate head from background.

Plate 24 Queen's tears (*Billbergia nutans*). Studio, with direct flash and extension tubes. ×2

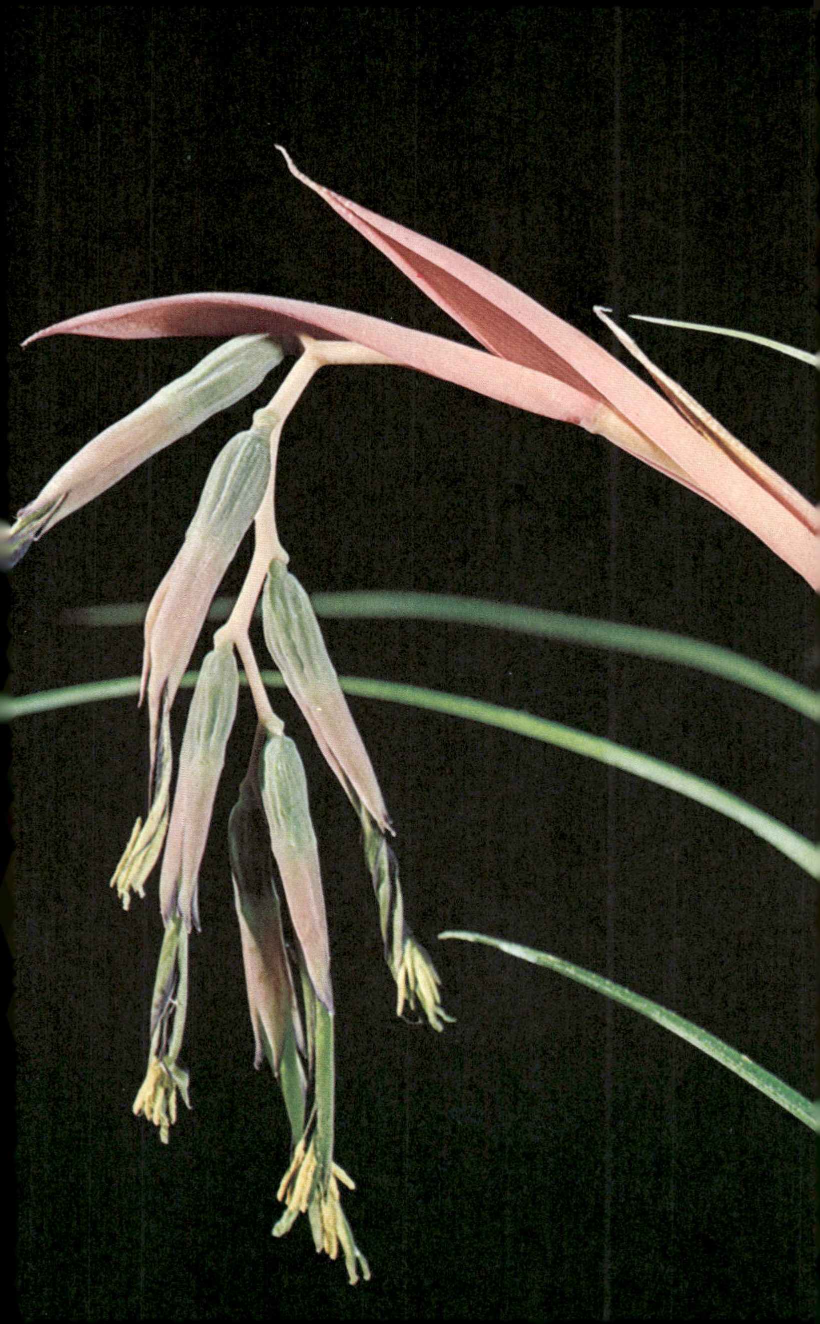

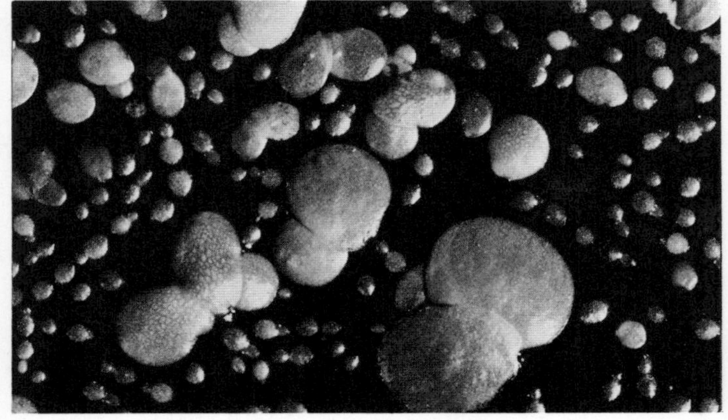

Fig. 4.4 Three species of duckweed, including *Wolffia arrhiza* – Britain's smallest flowering plant. Studio, aquarium with one oblique flash. Extension tubes. ×2·5

Setting up aquaria A standard sized aquarium is not essential for photographing aquatic plants. Almost any sized container will do, but preferably it should be made of clear glass or Perspex. A container with a coloured interior is not suitable since it will throw an unnatural colour cast on to the plants. Floating plants can be photographed in a shallow container slightly larger than the chosen field of view. I use a series of different sized Perspex tanks for all such overhead photography. Unless the plants will completely carpet the entire surface, a background must be placed in the bottom of the tank beforehand. A layer of mud or sand is most natural, but a piece of uni-toned board or even paper is often an adequate alternative.

The camera must be firmly supported above the tank either by using a copying stand or copipod, or by reversing the head of a tripod. A copying stand with adjustable rack and pinion movements allows for quick and critical focusing, in the same way as a focusing slide can be used on any fixed camera support.

Reflections of the lens and any shiny parts of a camera on the water surface, can be eliminated by mounting a matt-black mask on the front of the camera. The size of the central hole in the mask should be large enough not to restrict the field of view at the maximum lens aperture, although usually the lens will be stopped down to increase the depth of field with close-ups.

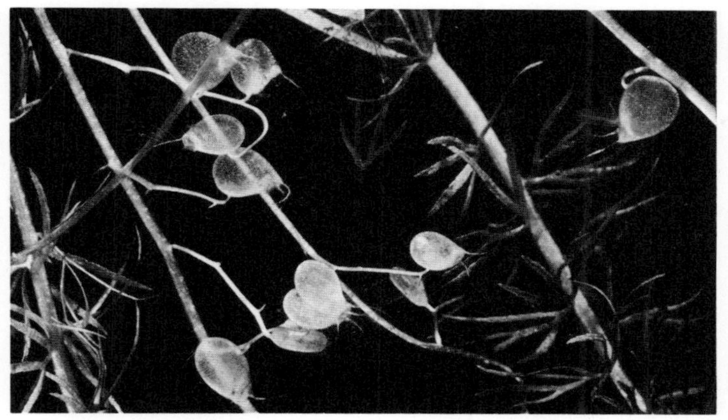

Fig. 4.5 Insectivorous bladderwort (*Utricularia intermedia*) showing underwater bladders. Studio, aquarium, with two flashes. Extension tubes. ×3

Lighting can be by available light shining through a window, by photofloods or by flashlight. With a rigid set up and static plants, diffuse daylight is ideal, since it will cast no shadows over the field of view and, providing long exposures are not used, it will give an acceptable colour rendering. Photofloods are not to be recommended as they generate so much heat. When working at night, use flashlight. Floating plants will have to be lit by directing the light source on to the surface. Do not mount the flash directly on to the camera, otherwise its reflection from the water surface will appear in the field of view. Instead, hold it well to one side at an angle of about 45° to the water. Use a reflector or a second flash to fill in on the opposite side of the tank (Fig. 4.4).

Submerged plants, such as the insectivorous bladderwort (Fig. 4.5) can be illuminated by shining lights down through the surface or through one side of the aquarium. One problem with submerged plants is that they release oxygen into the water as an end-product of photosynthesis. In bright light (sunlight or artificial) a constant stream of bubbles may be produced – especially from damaged stems or leaves. The solution is to postpone the photography and to cover the tank with a light-proof cover. Remember to tap or brush off any remaining bubbles before starting to photograph again, otherwise they will appear as distracting highlights in the picture.

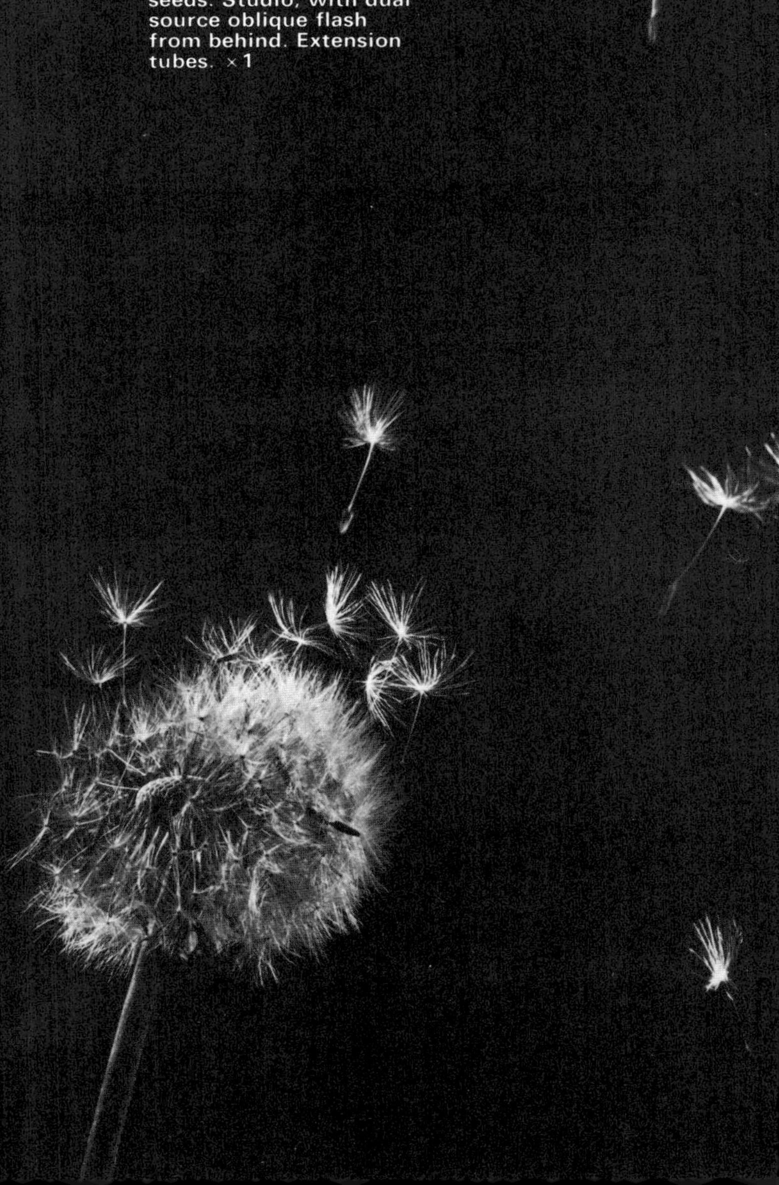

Fig. 5.1 Dandelion (*Taraxacum officinale*) dispersing seeds. Studio, with dual source oblique flash from behind. Extension tubes. ×1

The fruit and seeds produced by plants can be just as photogenic as the flowers themselves. After a flower has been pollinated and fertilized, the ovary develops into the fruit and the fertilized ovules become the seeds. Fruits which are dependent on their dispersal by animals eating them, produce attractive brightly coloured outer parts. Some fruits produce a powerful foetid smell as an additional lure.

In the field

Large and conspicuously shaped fruits are most suitable for photography in the field; whereas small fruits and especially seeds, are more suitable subjects for critical photography under controlled conditions indoors. Fruits are produced after a plant has flowered, so the best time for photographing them in temperate regions is in summer and autumn and in tropical regions, after the rains.

Solid subjects Both the shape and the colour should be clearly discernible in photographs of solid, smooth walled fruits such as hips and haws. Backlighting would be ineffective since they would then appear as dark objects without any indication of their three-dimensional form or their colour. Hence in direct sunlight the sun will need to be shining on the fruit from the front or from one side. Any direct light source, whether it be sunlight or flashlight will produce a highlight on the surface of shiny fruit. The reflection from the distant sun is usually less conspicuous and so more acceptable than a flash held at close range. Also, since the reflection of some flashes is rectangular, it is often preferable to use bounced flashlight. Diffuse lighting – either from the sun or a flash – can be created by using a diffusing screen as described on page 45. No obvious highlights will appear on the fruit which will look as if they had been photographed in the soft diffuse lighting of overcast days (Plate 12). Brightly coloured fruits are the easiest kinds to photograph in colour, since they automatically stand out from their surroundings, whether it be green foliage (Plate 12) or sky.

Hairy subjects Thistle and dandelion seeds have neither a conspicuous colour nor a solid shape. Photography of these delicate seeds requires a quite different approach. Delicate hairs are more clearly defined when they differ in tone from their background.

The combination of light and shade is ideal for showing hairy or spiny seeds or fruit; either by photographing them against the light (Plate 14) or by a shaft of sun spotlighting them against a background in shadow.

Seed dispersal As well as taking pictures of the mature fruit attached to the plant, a more exciting, but also more difficult approach, is to photograph the dispersal of seed (Fig. 5.1). The aim of seed production is to continue the propagation of a species. Distribution of seeds away from the parent plant not only helps to reduce overcrowding and competition for root space and light, but also ensures colonization of new areas.

Where seed dispersal is a hit or miss affair, large numbers of seeds tend to be produced, as for example by orchids which may have 74 million seeds per plant. The dust-like seed can be carried upwards in convection currents across the English Channel from France to Britain. Plants which have evolved some special dispersal mechanism, may also supply a store of food in the seed and so produce smaller numbers of larger seeds.

Many plants which grow beside freshwater or the sea have seeds which are dispersed by water. Water lily seeds are made buoyant by a slimy seed coat which traps air. When photographing seeds floating on water, the same problem of surface reflections will be encountered as already described for photographing aquatic plants on page 68.

Many more plants disperse their seeds by wind or with the help of animals, than by water. Wind buoys up and away these seeds and fruits with hair-like miniature parachutes. It sends winged fruits spiralling to the ground and shakes poppy and antirrhinum capsules so that their seeds are thrown out through the side openings like pepper out of a pepper pot. On windy days, hairy seeds are frequently seen being wafted along in the air, but from any one plant their release occurs intermittantly rather than continuously. The spread of the Oxford ragwort – an established alien on walls in Oxford since the late eighteenth century – has been accelerated by the wind-borne seeds entering railway carriages. Once inside, they may be carried for many miles before they float out of the windows.

Very fast reactions are needed to record on film the precise moment of dispersal of seeds from the plant. A higher success rate will be gained if a companion produces the wind by blowing on the plant at a predetermined moment. Either a fast shutter speed or flashlight will be essential for ensuring a crisp image of seeds dispersing (Fig. 5.1).

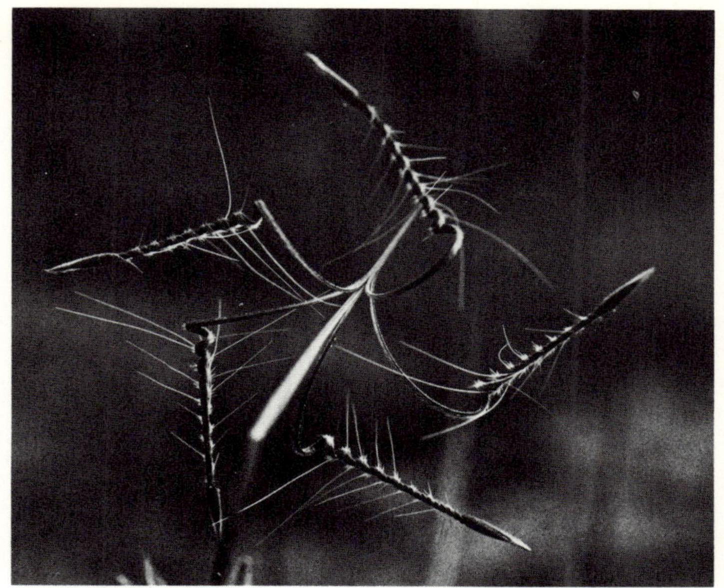

Fig. 5.2 Dehisced fruit of Mediterranean storksbill (*Erodium botrys*). Available light using close-up lens.

Mention has already been made of the way animals disperse seeds and fruits by eating the fleshy parts and rejecting or excreting the seeds; but they also unknowingly act as dispersal agents by accidentally picking up hooked fruits in their fur. Seeds of aquatic plants get carried from one water system to another in mud on the feet of aquatic birds. The seeds of several salt marsh plants have a mucilaginous coat which adheres to the feet of birds flying up from the marsh. Man disperses seeds both intentionally and unintentionally. Many medicinal and drug plants were introduced to Britain by monks, and can still be found today on the sites of old priories. Armies marching across Europe in Napoleon's time carried seeds of the barbed wire plant into several countries. Darwin grew some 70 species of grasses and other plants from the seed collected in his trouser turn-ups. Photographs of these clinging fruits are easy to take, since there is no problem of wind shake. However, an animal carrier might create problems by transporting the fruits out of the field of view.

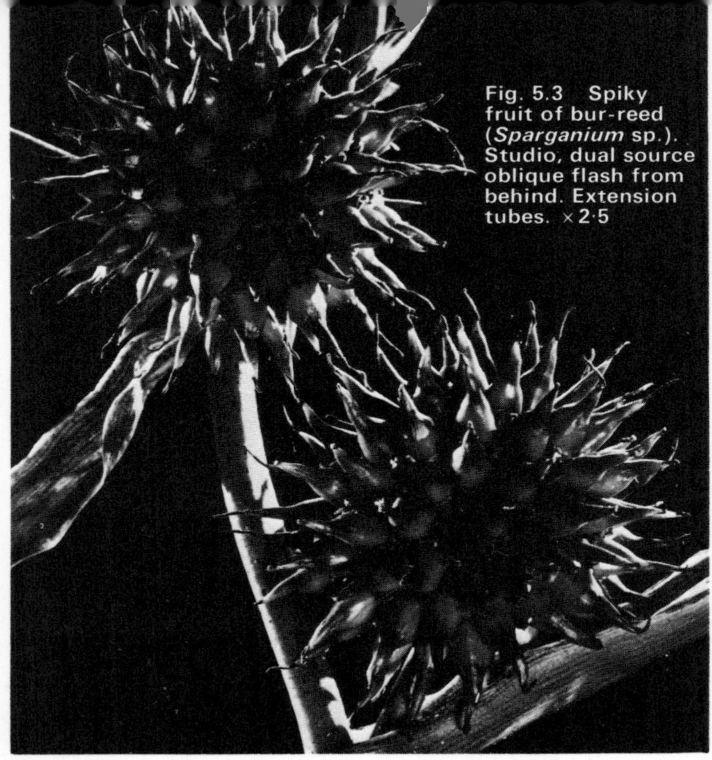

Fig. 5.3 Spiky fruit of bur-reed (*Sparganium* sp.). Studio, dual source oblique flash from behind. Extension tubes. ×2·5

Another method of seed dispersal is by means of the plant's own explosive devices. When the pods of legumes such as broom, gorse and vetch dry, they suddenly split open, the two halves curling back and flinging out the seeds. Cranesbills also disperse their seeds by the splitting of the ripe fruit. The long pointed capsule splits into five portions, each of which either curls back on itself, or twists spirally to disperse the seeds (Fig. 5.2). When ripe squirting cucumber fruits are knocked, they break free from the plant explosively flinging out their black seeds from the base. Photographing the precise moment of dehiscence of these explosive fruits in the field is even more difficult than dispersal by wind. *Shoddy aliens* are plants which are accidentally introduced into a country with the shoddy or wool waste used as manure on light sandy soils. The raw wool is scoured and the waste sold to market-gardeners and hop-growers. Originating from countries as far apart as Australia, South Africa, Uruguay and Brazil, the shoddy aliens can be identified by only a small group of specialist botanists who each year discover new alien species. Most of these plants produce hooked fruits or seeds which become entangled in the raw wool. Figure 5.2 was taken in a Hampshire apple orchard.

In the studio

Many fruits and seeds make ideal subjects for critical indoor photography, but in the interests of conservation only a few fruits, of even the commonest plants, should be collected.

Props When working on a table or a bench top the camera can either be supported on a small table-top tripod or on a tripod standing on the floor. For overhead views of flattened seeds or sectioned fruits, a copipod makes an ideal camera support.

The object of photographing seeds and fruits indoors is to obtain more detailed pictures about their structure than would be possible in the field, and so for these anatomical pictures uni-toned or uni-coloured backgrounds are ideal for isolating the subject. The colour or the tone should be selected for each subject; but black is particularly effective for photographing the majority of subjects in both colour and monochrome (Fig. 5.3). Sheets of paper or a piece of uncreased black velvet can be pinned on to hardboard and held vertically in place behind the subject. An erect subject can be supported either by holding the cut stem in a clamp stand or by pushing it into a heavy base such as a jar of sand, a block of plasticine or a flower arranger's spiky base. Unattached fruit or seeds will have to be photographed lying on a surface such as a sheet of glass (page 81) or the trough of a curved background.

Lighting Indoors, photographs can be taken using the available light shining through a conservatory or a window, or alternatively by photofloods or flashlight. Never mix different types of lighting; otherwise the results will show a false colour cast. Daylight colour film can be used with electronic flash as well as available light; but not with photofloods. With photofloods preferably use artificial light colour film; although daylight colour film can be used in conjunction with a colour conversion filter such as an 80B. Photofloods generate considerable heat and so are unsuitable for fleshy fruits, unless a heat filter is used.

The most suitable type of lighting to be used, and its direction will depend on each different subject. A continuous light source, like a spot light, is invaluable for checking the exact effect of light and shade on the subject before using flashlight. It will soon become apparent as the lighting is moved from in front, towards one side, that better modelling of the subject is achieved. Such oblique lighting, however, may create an unacceptable shadow on one side of the subject, which will have to be filled in by using a reflector or a second light source. With the direction of the light source in the same plane as the subject, extreme side lighting is produced – known as grazed lighting – which is ideal for showing details of textured fruits. Positioning of the light source should be such that distracting background shadows fall outside the field of view.

Two light sources can be used to provide dual source oblique lighting from in front or behind the subject. As in the field, back lighting is ideal for bringing out detail of fine hairs, or rim-lighting the outline of an intricate fruit against a black background (Fig. 5.3). The angle of the light or the flash can be reduced to provide a narrow beamed spot light by wrapping a tube of matt black paper around it. This directional beam will also reduce the chance of flare.

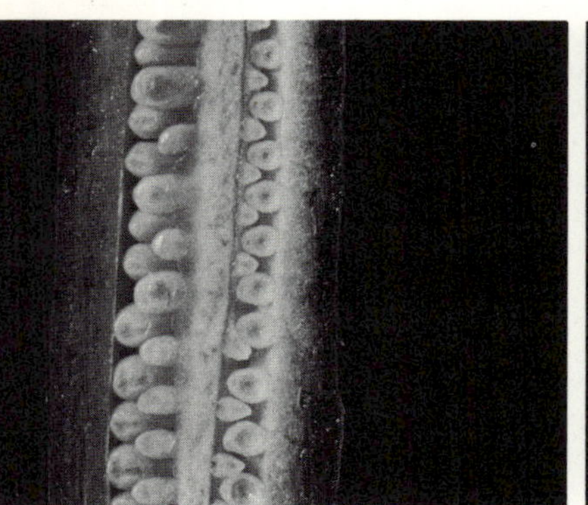

Fig. 5.4 Section through yellow iris (*Iris pseudacorus*) fruit showing seeds. Studio, grazed flash-light. Extension tubes. ×5.

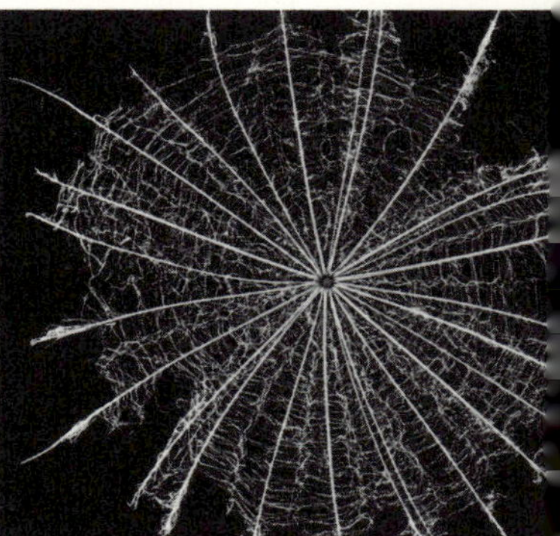

Fig. 5.5 Parachute from goat's-beard (*Tragopogon pratensis*) seed. Studio, dark field illumination. Extension tubes. ×2

For a given amount of extension, a greater magnification will be gained by using a shorter focal length lens. Thus a wide angle lens will give a larger magnification than a standard lens, which in turn will give a larger magnification than a long focus lens. But the shorter the focal length of the lens, the smaller the lens-to-subject distance will be. As already explained on page 19, the perspective will also change with the focal length of the lens, so that by direct viewing with an SLR camera, the ideal solution will be found for each subject. At magnifications of larger than life size (1:1), definition is improved by reversing the lens by attaching it to a reversing ring screwed on to the filter mount on the front of the lens. After a lens has been reversed, the automatic FAD coupling no longer operates.

Individual fruits can be photographed resting on a curved background or on a sheet of glass raised above the background. Lighting is not critical when using black velvet which absorbs all shadows, but it will have to be carefully positioned for all other backgrounds. A single direct light source directed down in front of and above the fruit resting on a pale background, will cause a shadow to fall behind the fruit. One or more side lights shining obliquely on to a fruit resting on a sheet of clear glass well above the background, will cast shadows outside the field of view. Alternatively, bouncing the light source will produce a softer edged shadow. As for aquarium photography, all shiny parts of the camera must be masked to avoid them being reflected in the glass. Plasticine is useful for supporting the base of an uneven fruit, especially if a cut surface needs to be held parallel to the camera, as in Plate 11.

Shiny fruits present the same problems indoors as in the field. Any direct light source will produce a highlight on the fruit, so that if more than one light is used, distracting multiple highlights will appear. Diffuse lighting, produced either by bouncing the light source or by shining it through a diffuser, will result in a much less conspicuous highlight. A diffusing cone can be made from translucent paper with the wide base encircling the fruit and the narrow top the camera lens. A light cone provides much more even lighting than a direct light source. For cameras without TTL metering, calculation of the correct exposure may be difficult however.

Dark field illumination is ideal for photographing hairy seeds and fruits, since it shows them brightly lit against a dark background (Fig. 5.5). A single seed will produce a clearer image than a cluster of seeds with their hairs overlapping. Place the seed on a glass plate about 15cm above a matt black background. Beneath the glass, position outside the field of view a ring of small torch or Christmas tree lights angled in towards the subject. None of the lights should shine directly into the camera lens. Their light rays reach the subject and are refracted so that they shine out around it, defining the smallest of details.

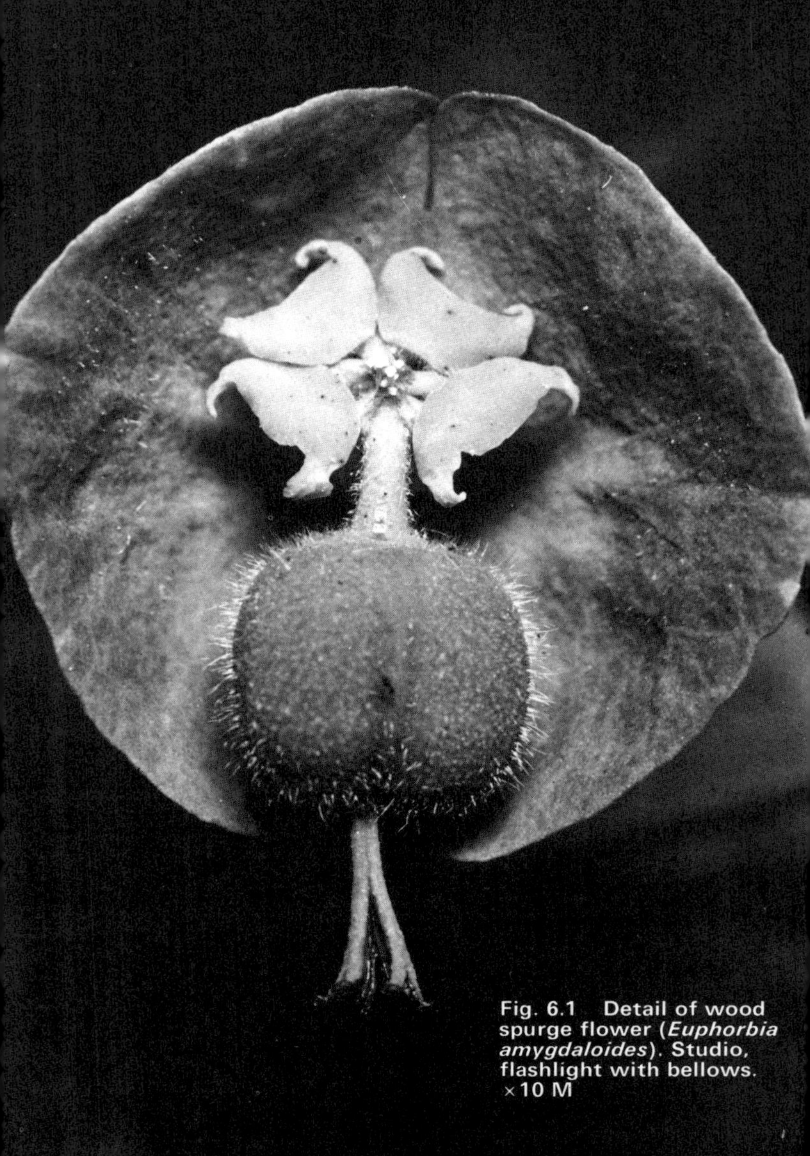

Fig. 6.1 Detail of wood spurge flower (*Euphorbia amygdaloides*). Studio, flashlight with bellows. ×10 M

Extreme close-ups of flowers and flower sections at magnifications greater than life size, are best taken in the studio. By selection of perfect specimens and critical use of the lighting, attractive detailed anatomical photographs can be made.

Collection

Only flowers which have a widespread distribution should be collected for studio photography; and even then just a few flowers or fruits cut from the plant. On land which is set aside as a Nature Reserve, collection of specimens is usually forbidden. Cut flowers sold by florists are ideal subjects for experimenting with lighting techniques. The most obvious methods for collecting flowers which are out of reach, are to use a pair of long armed pruners or a stepladder; but a botanist working in the tropics trained a monkey to scale trees and collect his flowers.

The standard container for collecting flowers is a vasculum, but any box or tin, or even a plastic bag will do, providing it is not carried around in direct sunlight for too long. Waterside plants with sappy stems soon begin to wilt after they are picked, unless they are immersed in water immediately after cutting. Any flowers with delicate petals are better collected in bud so that the petals will not become damaged in transportation. Flowers on woody stemmed plants survive long journeys better than soft stemmed annuals. Parts of plants should never be collected for photography unless they will survive the journey home and will be used for photography immediately after arrival.

Photography

Props for supporting both the camera and the specimen indoors, have already been described on page 79. The lighting techniques for indoor photography of fruits and seeds can also be applied to flowers. Photofloods emit considerable heat and so are not to be recommended.

Complete flowers on a rigid stem can have the cut stems immersed in water, in a vase or jam jar, with the stalk held in position with a ring of plasticine. Florists' spiky bases or Oasis are both useful supports for the bases of stems, in or out of water. Pot plants are easily adjusted in position for photography (Plates 15 and 24). Both cut flowers and pot plants can be photographed with a board or cloth background, but textured backgrounds or patterned wall-

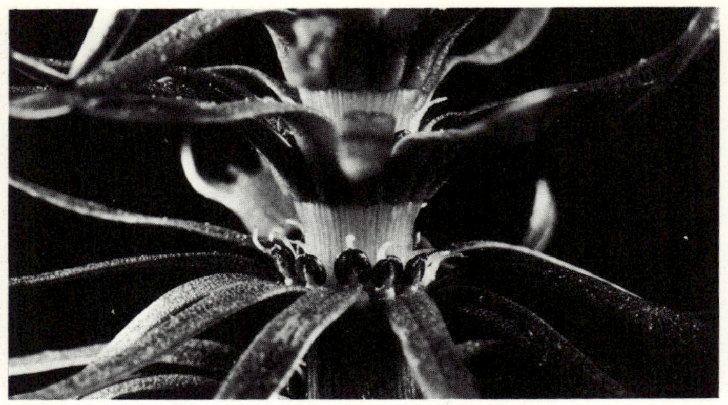

Fig. 6.2 Insignificant wind-pollinated flowers of mare's-tail (*Hippuris vulgaris*). Studio, dual source oblique flash from behind with fill-in frontal flash. Bellows. ×3 M

papers are unsuitable as natural history backcloths. Stemless solitary terminal blooms can be laid directly on the background (page 81), a sheet of glass (page 81) or floated on water.

Studio photographs can show the arrangement of individual flowers in an inflorescence, as well as the change in appearance of a flower with age. Rosebay willow herb, for example, is a typical protandrous flower in which the male stamens mature before the female stigma and style.

When commonplace flowers are photographed using full bellows extension, details not visible to the naked eye become apparent and the flowers take on a totally new appearance (Plates 21 and 22, Fig. 6.2). Notice how the back lighting has brought out the fine hairs on the dead-nettle stem. None of these plants, nor indeed any photographs in this book, were taken with a ring flash. This circular flash tube which surrounds the camera lens, provides uniform frontal lighting which, since it lacks modelling, gives a minimal pictorial effect. It is, however, useful for illuminating cavities inside flowers in a similar way to the special Medical Nikkor lens (with its built-in electronic ring flash encircling the front lens element) designed for photographing recessed areas. Ring lighting can be made slightly more directional by masking sections of the tube with aluminium foil.

Anatomy Details of floral parts and pollination mechanisms in

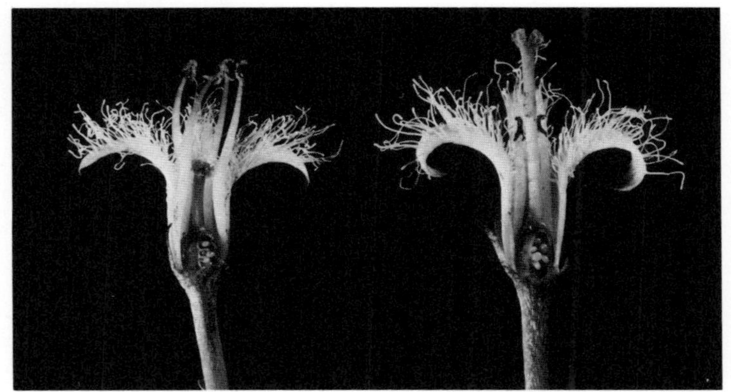

Fig. 6.3 Sections through short-styled (left) and long-styled (right) bogbean (*Menyanthes trifoliata*) flowers. Studio, dual source oblique flash. Extension tubes. ×2·5

flowers with a corolla tube partially or completely enclosed, can be shown only by sectioning. Longitudinal sections through the flowers of thrum and pin-eyed primrose and short and long-styled bogbean (Fig. 6.3) show how the relative positions of the stigma and the anthers prevent self-pollination. Sectioned flowers soon become flaccid, and so their photography will have to be undertaken as quickly as possible. The camera, background and light source should therefore be set up beforehand.

Time-lapse photography can illustrate the movements of the petals as a flower opens (Fig. 6.4). For scientific purposes, the interval between successive frames is usually kept constant, but could be varied if a purely pictorial effect is sought. Time-lapse photography can be done with a basic camera without special equipment. Both the camera-to-subject distance and the lighting must be kept constant throughout the sequence. Still time-lapse photographs are usually made on separate frames; but multiple exposures can be made on a single frame by recocking the shutter without winding on the film. The interval between exposures can either be timed manually, or automatically with a timing unit such as a mechanical clock or an electric timer. If an automatic timer is coupled to a motorized camera, the set-up can be left to run unattended. The time interval between successive frames will have to be determined on the basis of preliminary direct observations.

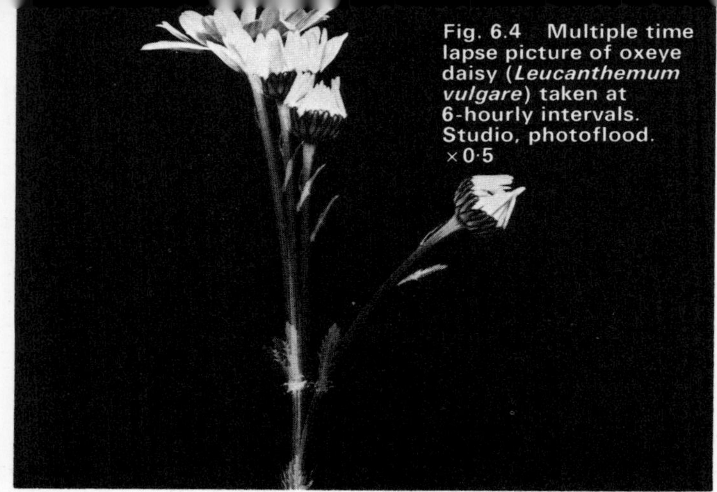

Fig. 6.4 Multiple time lapse picture of oxeye daisy (*Leucanthemum vulgare*) taken at 6-hourly intervals. Studio, photoflood. ×0·5

Pollination mechanisms Pollination is the transference of pollen from male anthers to the female stigma. Self-pollination is when this occurs within a single flower, and cross-pollination is when the pollen of one flower is transported to the stigma of another of the same species. Wind-pollinated flowers tend to be small and insignificant, often completely lacking any petals (Fig. 6.2), and without scent or nectar. Large quantities of small pollen grains are produced, which are easily carried in air currents. Detailed photographs of wind-pollinated flowers, which are typically well exposed to the wind, can be taken more easily indoors than out in the field. Insect pollinated flowers tend to be large and showy with brightly coloured petals, and are usually scented. The large, sticky pollen grains readily adhere to visiting insects. Photographs of insect visitors to flowers are more suitable subjects for photography in the field, where insects are more likely to undergo their typical behaviour patterns. Flowers which are pollinated by night-flying moths present a distinct challenge to the entomological or botanical photographer who aspires to taking purely natural pictures.

Ultra-violet light Many apparently uni-toned flowers show a distinct pattern when they are photographed with an ultra-violet emitting light source, with all visible light rays filtered out. Figure 6.5 compares an evening primrose flower photographed by white light and by ultra-violet light. Both the mercury vapour lamps used by entomologists to attract moths, and sunlamps emit ultra-violet light. The 125-watt entomological lamp, which must be used with the correct choke, takes several minutes to reach its maximum output. Do not look directly at this light; shield your eyes either with a hand or else by wearing the protective goggles sold by chemists for use with sun ray lamps. Ultra-violet pictures can be taken even in a lightened room, providing a Wood's glass filter is fitted on to the camera lens. This filter, which appears black, cuts out nearly all the visible wavelengths. Any ultra-violet pattern in the flower will not be seen until the film has been processed. There is a one in three chance that the chosen plant will have such a pattern, produced by differential absorption or reflection of the ultra-violet light by the flower. In the evening primrose, the dark centred petals and the stigma both absorb ultra-violet light and therefore stand out dark in contrast to the rest of the pale coloured flower which reflects ultra-violet light.

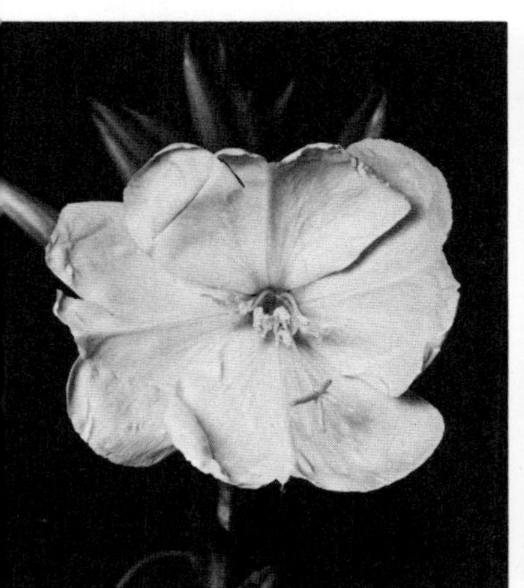

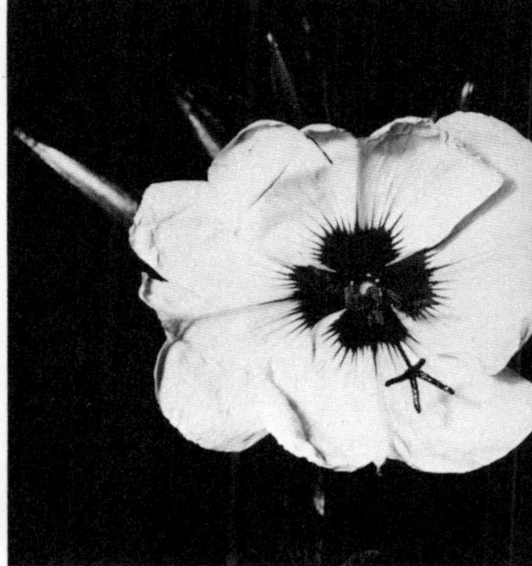

Fig. 6.5 Evening primrose (*Oenothera* sp.). Studio, with close-up lens. *Left:* in visible light. *Right:* in ultra-violet light.

To bees, these short wavelengths appear as the brightest colour of the whole spectrum, so to them the ultra-violet patterns are distinctly perceptible. The patterns presumably function as honey guides similar to those visible to the human eye.

The correct exposure for ultra-violet photography will have to be determined by trial and error. Small apertures should preferably be used, since the correct focus setting for a sharp image is not exactly the same as for visible light.

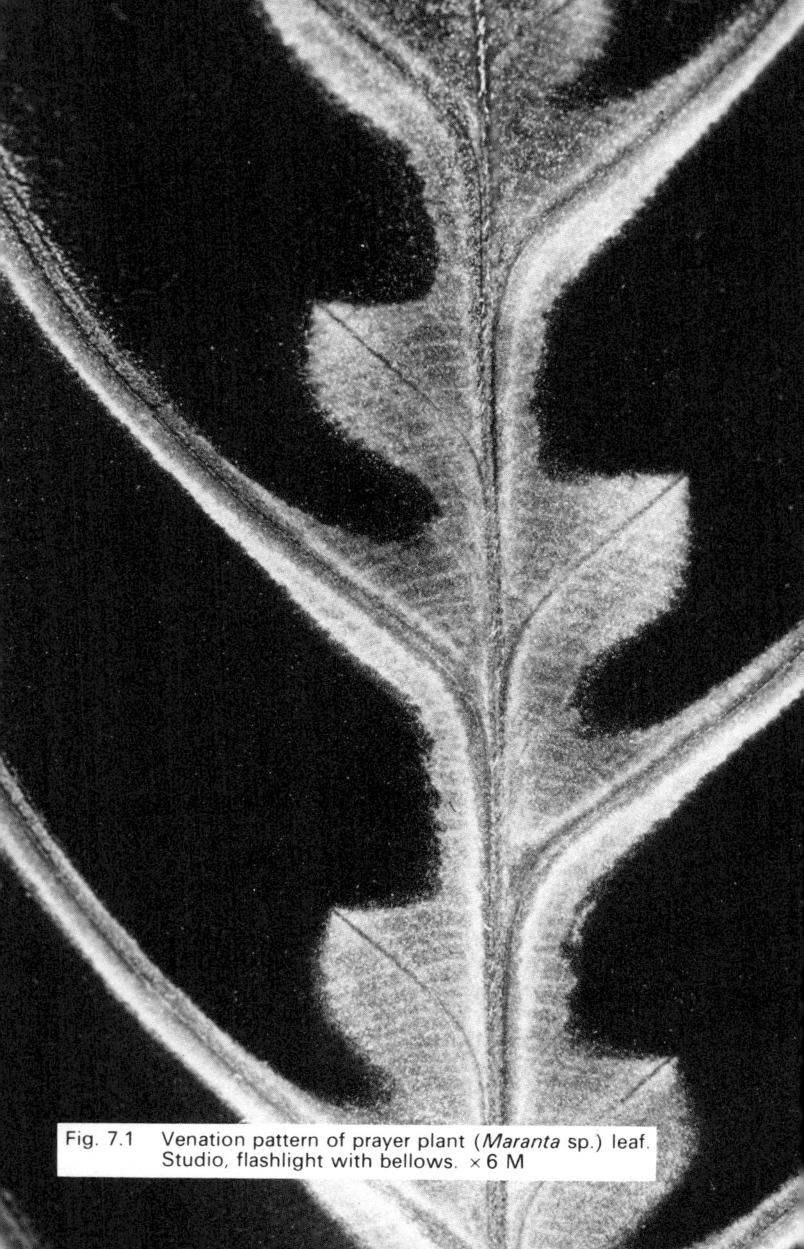

Fig. 7.1 Venation pattern of prayer plant (*Maranta* sp.) leaf. Studio, flashlight with bellows. ×6 M

CHAPTER 7 PATTERNS IN PLANTS

Plant patterns occur at all scales. They may be an ecological response to environmental changes. In tropical savanna country the dendritic pattern of the streams is picked out by the darker green of the gallery forests. Zonation patterns occur where there is a gradation of ecological change; for example, the landward end of a salt marsh is typically demarked by a distinct band of orache plants growing along the high water spring tide line. These plants are dispersed by water-borne seeds.

On a smaller scale, the distribution of individual plants may generate interesting patterns. Plants which spread by producing new plants at the end of runners, grow either in radiating patterns or in straight lines. The interaction or competition between plants results in different growth forms. For instance, dandelion plants on a lawn are quite distinct from dandelions growing in a hay field or on a wall. The growth pattern is the response of the plant's genetic make-up to the environment.

The spiral, alternate or opposite arrangements of leaves on a stem, produce the characteristic leaf mosaic which ensures the leaves overlap and shade each other as little as possible. Some flowers, are also arranged spirally on the stem. Climbing plants are supported either by the spiral growth of their stems or by tendrils entwining around other plants. Primitive flowers such as the magnolia and the water lily – amongst the oldest flowers in the fossil record – have a spiral arrangement of the petals and the stamens.

Individual leaves exist in a great range of shapes and patterns. Most simply, they can be circular, linear, lanceolate, oval or oblong. More elaborate leaf shapes are the lobed, palmate or pinnate forms. The largest round leaf in the world is the Victoria water lily, which can support the weight of a child. Paxton was the first person to successfully propagate this water lily in England from seed. The mechanical strength of the structure of the leaf's venation inspired him to use a similar design in the building of the Crystal Palace for the Great Exhibition of 1853. The main function of the leaf veins is to conduct water and nutrients from the roots via the stem, and also sugars manufactured in the leaf to other parts of the plant for use and storage. A secondary function is to provide the leaf with mechanical strength. Venation patterns of most leaves are best photographed using transillumination (page 53), except when they show a conspicuous pigmentation (Fig. 7.1).

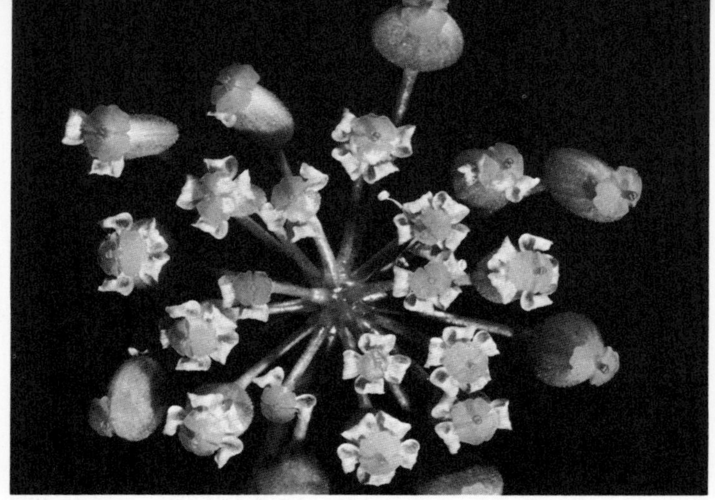

Fig. 7.2 Wild parsnip (*Pastinaca sativa*). Studio, flashlight with bellows. ×5 M

Other designs to look for are the colour patterns of leaves, especially of variegated plants, many of which are grown specially for their foliage. Thorns, spines and hairs have shapes that may require close-up or macro photography to bring out their design.

Plants such as the daisy, sunflower and water lily (Plate 8), which have radially symmetrical flowers, are examples of designs based on a circle. This symmetry is best shown by overhead photography with the film plane parallel to the flower. Daisy and dandelion heads are made up of many small flowers. The outer sterile ray florets are attractive, while the inner fertile disc florets produce the pollen and the ovules and, eventually, the seeds. A square format is ideal for photographing a circular flower, seed or fruit, since it can include the entire subject without much extraneous background (Plate 11 and Fig. 5.5). If a portion of these flat heads is photographed on a rectangular 35mm format so that it completely fills the frame (Plate 20), it will still convey the colour and pattern of the florets, without any distracting background encroaching on the picture.

The way in which a flowering shoot branches determines the type of inflorescence. The foxglove is a *raceme* which bears alternate stalked flowers, while the plantain is an example of a *spike* or a raceme with sessile flowers. Hogweed (Plate 23) and wild parsnip (Fig. 7.3) are both *umbels* with flowering stalks arising

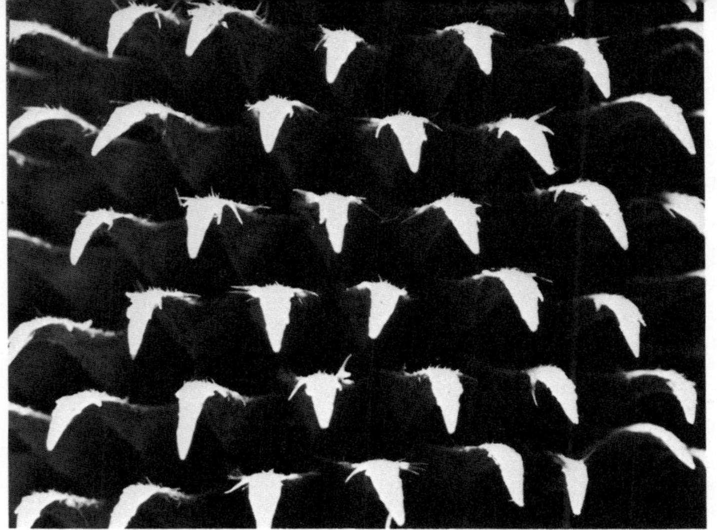

Fig. 7.3 Detail of Fuller's teasel (*Dipsacus fullonum sativus*) seed head used for bringing up pile on blankets. Studio, flashlight with bellows. ×6 M

from the same place on the stem. Both simple and compound umbels make ideal subjects for close-up designs. Less suitable for design pictures are the bilaterally symmetrical or zygomorphic flowers like the white dead-nettle (Plate 22), which have evolved elaborate systems to ensure cross-pollination by insects.

Close-ups of sectioned fruit with conspicuous seeds, show the arrangement of seeds inside the fruit (Fig. 5.4). Quite different designs will be seen in one kind of fruit by making transverse and longitudinal sections. Even a collection of dried seeds can make a picture worth taking.

The design of plant patterns always has some kind of biological significance. The photographer has the dilemma of whether to illustrate the design within its biological context, or to abstract it. The decision will be a personal one, depending on the individual's motivation. To many, a natural history picture should always be a biological record; to others, natural objects are merely sources of shape and pattern which can be exploited to create art forms. To me, the ideal solution is a compromise between these, since art is the basis of communication and the ultimate aim of all nature photographers is to communicate the fascination and beauty of the natural world.

APPENDICES

A PHOTOGRAPHIC GLOSSARY

Aperture Iris diaphragm of lens which controls amount of light reaching film. Calibrated in 'numerical apertures' (f numbers or stops) which change by a factor of 1.4 ($\sqrt{2}$) in one stop increments in series 1, 1.4, 2, 2.8, 4, ... 16, 22 . . . .
Artificial light film Colour filmstock for use with photoflood bulbs.
Ball-and-socket head Attached to tripod or other support to allow tilt and rotation of camera or flash.
Bellows Variable extension inserted between the lens and the camera body for close-up photography, allowing magnifications of greater than life size (1:1).
Bounced lighting Indirect diffuse lighting obtained by deflecting the light off a white board, wall or umbrella, above or to one side of the subject.
Close-up lens Attached to camera lens for close-up photography.
Colour cast Unnatural colouring due to using the incorrect film with a particular lighting (e.g. daylight film with photofloods), to reflection from a coloured surface or to reciprocity failure.
Colour compensating filter (CC) Corrects colour on colour films.
Contrast filter Strongly coloured filter used with monochrome films to lighten or darken a subject.
Conversion filter Used with colour films to correct overall colour balance, e.g. blue Wratten 80B used with daylight colour films and photoflood lighting; and orange Wratten 85 used with artificial light colour films in daylight.
Copipod Camera support with four legs used for overhead photography, especially copying work.
Dark field illumination Transmitted lighting, by which the subject appears brightly lit against a black background.
Depth of field Zone of sharp focus behind and in front of plane of focus. Increased by using a smaller aperture or by decreasing the image size.
Diaphragm See Fully automatic diaphragm and Preset diaphragm.
Diaphragm shutter Iris type shutter which allows synchronization with electronic flash at all speeds.
Diffuse lighting Soft lighting which produces soft edged shadows, and least obvious highlights on shiny objects.
Dioptre Unit expressing power of a lens. It is the reciprocal of the focal length in metres.
Electronic flash Reusable flash which produces an instantaneous discharge in a gas-filled tube.
Exposure The combination of shutter speed and lens aperture used to produce a good negative or transparency for a given film at a particular light intensity.
Extension tubes Inserted between the camera body and the lens for close-up photography. Automatic tubes retain the fully automatic diaphragm mechanism.
Film speed Relative sensitivity of a film to light, expressed as an ASA or a DIN rating. 'Slow' films have a low rating and require more light than 'fast' films.
Filter Alters the nature of light passing through the lens to the film, by absorbing particular wavelengths.
Flare Bright spots or patches formed by strong light reflections inside the lens, when the camera is pointed towards a light source. Flare can be reduced by using a lens hood or a multi-coated lens.
Focal plane shutter Camera shutter positioned immediately in front of the film plane, made of fabric or metal blinds.
Focus Adjusting the lens-film distance so that the subject image appears sharp on the film plane.
Focusing slide Used mounted on a tripod, it allows the camera to be moved towards or away from the subject for critical focusing in close-up work, without altering the magnification.

Frame A single exposure amongst a series on a film.
Fully automatic diaphragm (FAD) Remains at full aperture until shutter release is operated, when the diaphragm closes down to the preselected aperture.
Grazed lighting (Textured lighting) Extreme low angled oblique lighting used for emphasizing texture.
Ground spike Camera support for ground level subjects, the base of which is pushed into the ground.
Guide number (Flash factor) When divided by the subject distance, indicates correct aperture (or vice versa). Does *not* apply for close-ups.
Haze filter Absorbs ultra-violet radiation. It is especially useful when working at altitude or near large expanses of water.
Incident light reading Measures the light falling on the subject. The light meter, with a diffuser attached, is pointed in the subject-to-camera direction.
Lens hood Projects in front of lens. It reduces the possibility of back lighting striking the front surface of the lens and thereby causing flare.
Long focus lens Has a focal length greater than the standard lens, and increases the camera-to-subject distance for a given image size.
Macro lens A lens with built-in extension allowing magnifications of up to 0·5 without using extension tubes or bellows.
Monopod A single legged camera support.
Parallax The discrepancy between the image seen through the viewfinder, or the upper lens of a TLR camera, and the image recorded on the film.
Pentaprism Five-sided prism used in SLR cameras to ensure the image is correctly orientated in the viewfinder.
Perspective correcting lens Special wide angle lens used for correcting converging verticals, by off-centring the lens.
Photoflood Artificial light used for studio work for monochrome and artificial light colour films.
Polarizing filter Used to reduce distracting reflections from water and glass or wet and shiny surfaces. It also darkens a blue sky.
Preset diaphragm (PD) A non-automatic diaphragm in which the iris must be stopped down manually to the preset aperture.
Reciprocity failure According to the Reciprocity Law, exposure equals light intensity × time. With short ($<1/_{1000}$ second) and long ($>1/_2$ second for colour films) exposures the Law fails, film speed is lost and the colour balance shifts.
Reflected light reading Measures the light reflected from the subject. The light meter is directed away from the camera towards the subject.
Reflex camera Has ground glass screen for critical composition and focusing. Twin lens reflex (TLR) cameras have two lenses, one for viewing and one for taking, while single lens reflex (SLR) cameras have one lens only.
Reversing ring Accessory for mounting the lens on the camera body in the reverse position for macrophotography.
Ring flash Electronic flash which encircles the camera lens. Provides frontal lighting in extreme close-ups.
SLR See Reflex camera.
Standard lens Has a focal length approximately equal to the diagonal of the negative or transparency, giving an angle of view of 45–50°.
Stop (f number) Numerical aperture of lens iris diaphragm which controls the intensity of light reaching the film.
Synchro-sunlight Balanced combination of sunlight and flashlight.
TLR *See* Reflex camera.
TTL (Through the lens) meter Reflected light meter built into an SLR camera which measures the light passing through the lens.
Transmitted light Light which passes through the subject.
Ultra-violet light Invisible short wave-lengths which produce an image on monochrome or colour films, when all visible light rays are excluded with a filter.
Wide angle lens Short focal length lens giving a wider angle of view (greater than 50°) than a standard lens used from the same position.

B EQUIPMENT CHECK-LIST FOR FLOWER PHOTOGRAPHY

Basic field equipment

Camera with standard lens (50mm for 35mm format) / (80mm for 6 × 6cm format) with lens hood
Light meter (if camera does not have TTL metering)

Films
Tripod
Ground spike
Spare batteries for TTL meter
Cable release
Lens tissues and lens brush
Close-up lenses and/or extension tubes
Gadget bag or foam-padded rucksack
Plastic sheet for kneeling
Scissors
Wire for tying back branches
Hand lens
Pocket tape measure
Notebook or pocket tape recorder

Additional field equipment

Medium long focus lens (105 or 135mm for 35mm format) / (150 or 250mm for 6 × 6cm format) with lens hood

Macro lens
Bellows
Focusing slide
Flash (bulb or electronic)
Right-angled flash bracket
A monopod or spike with flash shoe
Waist level or right angle viewfinder
Torch for focusing in dark wood
Wind shield
Compass
Contrast filters
Polarizing filter
Stepladder
Reflector
Umbrella
Binoculars

Additional studio equipment

Table-top tripod
Camera cradle
Copying stand
Clamp stands
Black velvet
Board backgrounds
Spotlights
Photofloods
White card
Plasticine
Sand
Sheets of glass
Ring flash
Reversing ring
Plastic seed trays
Flower-arrangers' pinholders
Light box
Aquarium

C THE NATURE PHOTOGRAPHERS' CODE OF PRACTICE

All photographers working in Britain should read the following leaflets:

1) *The Nature Photographers' Code of Practice*, produced by the Association of Natural History Photographic Societies. Copies can be obtained from the RSPB, The Lodge, Sandy, Bedfordshire, SG19 2DL, by sending a stamped addressed envelope.

2) *A code of conduct for the conservation of wild plants*, produced by the Botanical Society of the British Isles. Copies can be obtained from the Hon. General Secretary, BSBI, c/o Department of Botany, British Museum (Natural History), Cromwell Road, London SW7 5BD.

D BOOKS FOR FURTHER READING AND IDENTIFICATION

★ Extensively illustrated with photographs.
† For identification of flowers.

★ Angel, Heather, *Nature Photography: Its art and techniques*, Fountain Press/M.A.P., Kings Langley, 1972.

★† Barneby, T. P., *European alpine flowers in colour*, Nelson, London, 1967.

★† Bramwell, D. and Bramwell, Z., *Wild Flowers of the Canary Islands*, Thornes, London, 1974.

† Bursche, E. M., *A handbook of water plants*, Warne, London, 1971.

† Butcher, R. W., *A new illustrated British flora*, 2 vols. Leonard Hill, London, 1961.

† Clapham, A. R., Tutin, T. G. and Warburg, E. F., *Flora of the British Isles*, 2nd ed., Cambridge University Press, 1962.

Corner, E. J. H., *The Life of Plants*, Weidenfeld and Nicholson, London, 1964.

★† Craighead, J. J., Craighead, F. C. and Davis, R. J., *A Field Guide to Rocky Mountain Wildflowers*, Houghton Mifflin Co., Boston, 1963.

Dandy, J. E., *List of British Vascular Plants*, Brit. Mus. (Nat. Hist.), London, 1958.

Dony, J. G., Rob, C. M. and Perring, F. H., *English names of wild flowers*, Butterworth, London, 1974.

† Duperrex, A., *Orchids of Europe*, Blandford, London, 1961.

★ Eliovson, S., *Discovering wild flowers of Southern Africa*, 2nd ed., Timmins, Cape Town, 1969.

Fitter, R. S. R., *Finding Wild Flowers*, Collins, London, 1971.

† Fitter, R. S. R., Fitter, A. and Blamey, M., *The Wild Flowers of Britain and Northern Europe*, Collins, London, 1974.

Grigson, Geoffrey, *A Dictionary of English Plant Names*, Allen Lane, London, 1974.

★† Harris, T. Y., *Alpine plants of Australia*, Angus & Robertson, Sydney, 1970.

† Hodgson, M. and Paine, R., *A Field Guide to Australian Wild Flowers*, Rigby, Adelaide, 1971.

† Hubbard, C. E., *Grasses*, 2nd ed., Penguin Books, Middlesex, 1968.

† Huxley, A., *Mountain flowers in colour*, rev. ed., Blandford, London, 1973.

† Kidd, M. M., *Wild flowers of the Cape Peninsula*, 2nd ed., O.U.P., Cape Town, 1973.

† Martin, W. Keble, *The Concise British Flora in Colour*, Ebury Press, London, 1965.

★ Milne, L. and Milne, M., *Living Plants of the World*, Nelson, London, 1967.

† Parsons, M. E., *The wild flowers of California*, Dover, New York, 1966.

Perring, F. H. and Walters, S. M., *Atlas of the British Flora*, Nelson, London, 1962.

† Peterson, R. T. and McKenny, M., *A Field Guide to Wild Flowers of Northeastern and north-central North America*, Houghton Mifflin Co., Boston, 1968.

★† Polunin, O., *Flowers of Europe*, Oxford University Press, London, 1969.

★† Polunin, O. and Smythies, B. E., *Flowers of South-West Europe*, Oxford University Press, London, 1973.

★ Proctor, M. and Yeo, P., *The pollination of flowers*, Collins, London, 1973.

★† Salmon, J. T., *New Zealand flowers and plants in colour*, A. H. and A. W. Reed, Wellington, 1970.

★ Sire, Marcel, *Secrets of plant life*, Collins, London, 1967.

† Summerhayes, V. S., *Wild orchids of Britain*, Collins, London, 1951.

† Thommen, E., *Atlas de Poche de la Flore Suisse*, 2nd ed., Editions Birkhäuser, Bâle, 2 vols., 1961.

★ Tosco, U., *The world of mountain flowers*, Orbis, London, 1974.

† Tutin, T. G., *et al.* (eds.), *Flora Europaea*, Cambridge University Press, Vol. 1, 1964; Vol. 2, 1968; Vol. 3, 1972.

The New Naturalist Library, Collins, London, includes several useful books, e.g. *Flowers of the Coast*, *Wild Flowers of Chalk and Limestone* and *Mountain Flowers*.

INDEX

Numbers in **bold** type refer to illustrations

Printed in England by W. S. Cowell Ltd, Ipswich